RIDE IT!

The Complete Book of

SPEEDWAY

Printed and bound in England by the publishers

Published by
HAYNES PUBLISHING GROUP
SPARKFORD   YEOVIL   SOMERSET   BA22 7JJ   ENGLAND

a FOULIS MOTORCYCLING BOOK — ISBN   0   85429   210   1

Editor   Jeff Clew
Production/Design   Tim Parker
Illustration   Terry Davey

Distributed in North America by
Haynes Publications Inc.
861 Lawrence Drive
Newbury Park
California 91320

Telephones (213) 889 - 5400   (805) 498 - 6703

RIDE IT!

The Complete Book of

SPEEDWAY

Cyril May

Contents

Foreword

There has long been a need for a really definitive book about speedway racing, which is soon to celebrate its introduction into Britain fifty years ago. It seems incredible that what was regarded initially as a new diversion for amateur motorcyclists captivated the nation almost overnight and in a comparitively short time ranked as the sport with the second largest following, displaced only by football.

I am glad that I was invited to contribute this Foreword, for I was one of those fortunate enough to become involved with speedway racing (or dirt track racing as it was then called) in the early days. At that time a young South London motorcycle enthusiast, I rode for Preston, before leaving to seek my fortune nearer home with the Wimbledon team. It was a good move too, for in 1933 I became one of the first riders to amass one hundred league points in a season. But later I had my fair share of misfortune too - all part of a speedway rider's life. Fate is the unknown factor in every success story.

It is fitting that Cyril May should have written this fascinating story because he must surely rate as one of our leading authorities on the history and development of the sport. That he has succeeded in capturing the atmosphere so vividly is no exaggeration, for I soon found myself reliving the oft-forgotten past and savouring something of that unique era of long ago. The photographs alone, many of which have never been published before, made many of the early meetings seem as though they had been held only yesterday.

This really is *THE COMPLETE BOOK OF SPEEDWAY* and enthusiasts the whole world over will be grateful to Cyril May for presenting it in such an authoritative, attractive and readable manner.

CLAUDE RYE

Preface

When it was suggested that I should write a book on the history of British speedway racing, and how the sport originated, I agreed immediately. But when I really got down to the work, I soon found that to do the job properly, at least fifty volumes would have to be written! Of course, one volume it had to be and, needless to say, endeavouring to get 'gallons into a whisky glass' has been no easy matter, although I have derived a great amount of pleasure in its compilation.

Alas, of necessity, many facets of the speedway story have, regretfully, had to be omitted. But, nevertheless I trust you will find this, not only a fair study, but an interesting one.

My aim has been to give you something out of the common run, and, moreover the majority of the various illustrations have never previously been published.

I only hope that I have succeeded.

CYRIL MAY
Devizes
Wiltshire

Acknowledgements

Obviously I am equally grateful to all those who have kindly supplied me with photographs for this book, to supplement some of my own. I have therefore listed them in alphabetical order. May I express my thanks once again.

The late Frank Arthur   Miss Eva Askquith   Cecil Bailey   Jeff Clew   Mrs Kitty Cole
Leonard Cole   John Comerford   Mrs Bobbie Datson   Bill Davies   Del Forster   William Frogley
Roland Groom   Harley-Davidson Motor Co, Inc   Mrs Kay Hill-Bailey   Johnnie Hoskins   Vic Huxley
Bob Jones   Billy Lamont   Charlie May   Dave McMahon   Gary Morse   *Motor Cycle*
George Newton   Rodney Pashley   Mike Patrick   Wal Phillips   Mrs Emily Watson   Alf Weedon
Weslake and Co, Ltd   John Willmott   Wright Wood

Introduction

Often overlooked is the fact that speedway racing depends for its appeal on nothing beyond a clean sport and the thrills it has to offer. It has, of course, been built up, once again, on the unbounded enthusiasm of daring riders, of never-to-be-discouraged promoters, and of all the thousands of supporters.

Speedway racing certainly affords excitement; the sight of a group of riders hurtling round the track; a failing motor; a favourite gaining ground; a spectacular broadside, all provide real, true excitement. To provide this entertainment men and young lads gamely risk broken limbs, even their lives. Unfortunately, racing is not immune from such tragedies, though fortunately they rarely occur.

It is a sport which attracts all types of people for different reasons; it is held in the healthy open air; and above all, it is essentially a family sport. Mother, father and children, rich or poor, haughty or humble, all find extreme satisfaction in this exhilarating sport of ours. Is it no small wonder that speedway racing is so popular; interest is increasing every season, and a proportion of the vast crowds that existed in the immediate post-war years seems to be coming back.

Good clean, healthy, satisfying entertainment is speedway's motto. Sportsmanship is continually making itself manifest in the great game. A closely contested race often provides a hearty handshake; a rider loans some of his expensive spare parts and sometimes his complete machine to another one less fortunate.

Racing is not without its display of heroics. Many times a rider swerves suddenly to miss a fallen opponent; often he crashes himself and is possibly injured. A rider after finishing a race will perhaps return for a fallen competitor to give him a lift back to the pits. These kindly gestures help us to feel very proud to belong to such a sport.

All, without exception, are great-hearted fellows and, together with those who, by reason of limited space are regretfully not included in this Book, have brought nothing but the highest credit to the sport.

The human touch comes very much into speedway racing. Every enthusiast likes to feel that he is a close friend of the riders he most admires; there's none of that impersonality which exists in so many other sports. This, of course, is as it should be, and it has always been pleasant to see how readily the boys react to the approaches of their admirers. No stand-offish rider would get very far in the sport however good his ability.

The Auto-Cycle Union's rules and regulations attached to racing are carefully thought out; they are clear and emphatic and in the general craving for excitement and thrills, the public's safety is not forgotten. If an accident takes place, the race is immediately stopped by the Steward and first-aid men are quickly on the spot.

This virile sport has an open way ahead and with every reason we may suppose that the success of this 1976 season will overshadow that of its predecessors.

Yes, the future looks very bright for speedway racing. May you all enjoy the very best of it ... I'm sure you will!

1 The early days

Today, the majority of the thousands of spectators thronging the various tracks to watch the thrilling display of daring riders are not aware just exactly how speedway racing started; how desperate at various times was the struggle to keep it going; how grim were the trials and tribulations which many managements underwent, all of which had great faith in the sport and who were determined that this spectacular pastime should swell to greater proportions. The whole story of speedway racing's rise from primitive beginnings to periods of great popularity is a fascinating one, and an exciting tale of triumph over prejudice and criticism.

This, then is the story ...

The general belief that speedway racing originated in Australia is certainly a fallacy, and it may come as a surprise to many to hear that it was quite popular in America as early as 1909. The late R.M.Samuel, more affectionately known as Sammy and former Editor for a considerable number of years of *Speedway News,* was in close touch with the sport through business reasons, and he thought it quite likely that it had been going on even earlier.

There was very keen competition between such manufacturers as the Harley-Davidson, Excelsior, Indian, Peerless and Cleveland companies. Professional riders were retained by these and other firms and race meetings on improvised tracks were regular attractions at the big State Fairs which in those days flourished in the extreme. As to the circuits, these were quite big and no attempt was made to surface them. Thus the term dirt track racing came into existence.

But another story survives — although confirmation as to its authenticity is not available — that a first recorded motorcycle race meeting on a circuit with a loose dirt surface was staged at Pietermaritzburg (South Africa) in the spring of 1907.

The immense popularity that motorcycle racing gained in the early 'twenties in the United States was entirely due to fierce competition on half-mile dirt tracks. These courses had been built originally for horse-trotting and pacing races and the oval tracks were dotted around the country from Maine to California.

During the ascendency of the racing car, the tracks lay idle for a while; the spectator stands and the fences became decayed, while the courses themselves became overgrown with grass. Then, with fearless riders in the saddle, racing motorcycles were set loose upon the neglected surfaces, and like a prairie fire, competition between the various makes of machines swept through America.

Many of the tracks were a mile or even more to the lap, but the majority were half-milers and through Indiana and Ohio, race meetings were popular to the extreme. At times there were no less than three meetings within a radius of about eighty miles in Ohio on the same day and each one drew fantastic crowds.

But the tracks with their loose, dusty surfaces and dangerous fences, inevitably caused many fatalities although a rule restricting engine capacities had tended to decrease the accidents. With a group of riders struggling for the lead, heavy clouds of dust hung over the tracks and in spite of precautions such as the spraying of light oil or calcium chloride on the surface, there still remained a peculiar haze through which it was difficult to see. But the sport thrived ... and thrived. It was super-thrilling and super-exciting with the intrepid riders gambling with the undertaker all the time.

The American racing machines were of special design; fragile, delicate, short-lived and impracticable for use as ordinary roadsters. They had been over-developed until the machines were capable of speeds far in excess of the

Dirt track racing was an off-shoot of the famous American board racing in the 1920s

The legendary wrecking crew at the Dodge City Speedway in 1920. From left to right; Maldwyn Jones, Fred Ludlow, Ralph Hepburn, Jim Davis, Ray Weishaar, Otto Walker and Walter Higley

limits of the safety of the tracks, with of course, the exception of a few two-mile dirt tracks and the famed board tracks. There was the inevitable element of recklessness, for the winner was usually the rider who used his magneto cut-out button the least.

Many American motorcycle manufacturers spent vast amounts of money in supporting the various race meetings, such as the Indian and Harley-Davidson Companies, and alas, many valuable lives had been lost in the never-ending quest for speed ... and still more speed.

On August 14, 1921, Albert Burns, better known as ''Shrimp'', and one of the best riders in the States, crashed into a pole on the Toledo (Ohio) mile dirt track and was unfortunately killed. He was the mainstay of the Indian racing team, and some three weeks before, had raced against the cream of the Harley-Davidson riders, riding eight-valve machines on the mile dirt track at Kenosha (Wisconsis). Single-handed he had beaten them in three events. It was a magnificent performance.

During the 1921 racing season, for a time it seemed as though sentiment favoured having machines of 1,000cc barred from competition, except on dirt tracks of more than a mile to the lap, but as long as the motorcycle trade dominated the M and ATA Competition Committee, this outlawing appeared to be unlikely.

However at Chicago an attempt was made to incorporate a 600cc class, which would develop racing between the various sports models. But the manufacturers were not interested in developing another size of racing engine. That the big 1,000cc motors had developed beyond the safety limits was proved by a look at the M and ATA records list for 1921. On the one mile dirt track at Syracuse, New York, Fred Ludlow on a Harley-Davidson won six short distance Championships, averaging over 80mph, in the races under ten miles and 78mph, in the twenty-five and fifty-mile events!

Dirt track racing was flourishing in Canada too, especially at the Toronto circuit, a comparatively small track which made for closer racing, and sensational finishes on such tracks were certainly very frequent. Events with at least five sidecar outfits competing in one race caused great excitement and immense enthusiasm; there were banking sidecars too.

In America on the one mile track at Maxwellton, St. Louis, Gene Walker on a 1,000cc Indian created new records from one to ten miles. His mile was clocked at 85 mph; the five miles at 83mph, and the ten miles at 80mph. In the sidecar races too, tremendously high speeds were being accomplished on one mile tracks. Floyd Dreyer, with an Indian-Flexi outfit set up new figures at the Toledo track, the day that ''Shrimp'' Burns was so sadly killed. Floyd's average speed for the one mile was around the 70mph mark, and from that distance on, up to twenty-five miles he circled the course averaging a fantastic 65mph.

Harley-Davidson's dirt track racer of 1920 — very basic motorcycle with no exhausts. Note the pedal-type footrest and the retention of the rear stand

These high-powered super machines obviously needed super riders, and the fearless Americans certainly rose to the occasion. With these heavy models with "vertical" handlebars and 1,000cc power-plants, there was hardly any broadsiding — perhaps just a little. The technique of cornering was to roll around the bend, with a little throttle and the wheels in line, similar to the road-racing style.

'The Roaring Twenties' they called them and no other title could so aptly apply to that particular era. Among the aces were: Otto Walker, Walter Higley, Ray Weishaar, Ralph Hepburn, Jim Davis, Fred Ludlow, Gene Walker and Maldwyn Jones, while the "banking" sidecar exponents were: Floyd Dreyer, Bill Minnick, and "Jiggs" Price with their Flexi outfits. There was very strong rivalry between the Harley-Davidson, the Indian and the Excelsior factory teams who toured the country like a circus, from track to track.

The many fatalities that had occurred were very distressing to the American official governing body of the motorcycle sport and by 1922 much more attention was being given to 500cc engined-machines in the interests of safety. Within two years, the monster thousands had been barred on all tracks. Incidentally, in 1922 there was not one single race meeting held on any other circuit but dirt track courses, and most of them were half-milers.

The introduction of smaller capacity motors, therefore, permitted a more spectacular method of cornering, and as the end of the season drew to a close all the top riders had mastered the method of controlling sliding, with 500cc models.

However, the credit for the invention of the broadside or pendulum skid in 1922 is given by the Americans to the renowned Maldwyn Jones, the Excelsior and Harley-Davidson rider, but during the year other 500cc aces had accomplished the new style too. They were the illustrious Eddie Brinck, Paul Anderson, Ralph Hepburn, Jim Davis, Gene Walker and others.

After two years had elapsed, the smaller engine machines (500cc) were being raced everywhere in the United States, and broadsiding was now the recognised riding style of rounding the bends of the dirt tracks the fastest way.

Towards the end of 1925, 350cc racing machines made their debut on the Milwaukee dirt track and created a great sensation. Hitherto, racing in America had been confined to the 500cc and 1,000cc classes, but with the introduction of the Harley-Davidson and Indian 350cc road models, special ohv machines were constructed for racing purposes. In the Harley range, these 21 cubic-inch "Peashooters" as they were named, averaged over 69mph, in five-mile races!

The annual Milwaukee race meeting crowds saw for the first time, these 350cc models in competition in America. Motorcycle racing history was in the making when these "Peashooters" were turned loose, and when the dust had cleared away they had firmly established themselves in the hearts of the riders, the dealers and the general public. The riders came into the pits with a smile of satisfaction, and had nothing but high praise for the way the "Peashooters" handled. They were in fact, only two seconds slower than the renowned five-hundreds. The riders were bunched all the time and finishes were extremely close.

After the 1,000 and 500cc events had terminated, the little "Peashooters" came out to do their five-mile stint. They started off in a pack and sounded like a bunch of bees as they went swarming into the bend, down the back straight, and into the next corner and still running like a bunch of eight-day clocks. First one and then the other would take the lead and the crowd was in an uproar; they had never seen anything quite like this before.

The stop watches showed a mile in forty-nine seconds! Hardly believable with those little things. James Davis would lead the pack, and then Eddie Brinck, until Jimmy retired which left Johnny Vance and Joe Petrali on the tail of Eddie, who eventually won an exceptionally close and well-fought race by the length of his moustache. Eddie Brinck then went on to win the ten-mile and fifteen-mile events.

It was a day to remember, and Walter Davidson and Bill Harley were overjoyed at the performance of their new "Peashooters" ... a slice of motorcycle history had certainly been made at Milwaukee dirt track.

Toledo, Kenosha, Syracuse, Maxwellton and Milwaukee. These were all dirt track circuits. These names meant speed. These names meant the growl and thunder of machines flat-out ... against each other; against the clock. Names that meant the clean sharp smell of hot racing oil, checkered flags, trophies, colour and excitement ... plus extraordinary amounts of skill and courage by brave riders with excellent reflexes, co-ordination and balance. Harley-Davidson machines with their factory riders were winning races at a phenomenal rate on the various dirt tracks. Road races and endurance events alike were dominated by stock pocket-valve and special eight-valve racing machines produced by HD. Back in 1920 both the stock and racing engines set speed records at Daytona Beach. The stock-pocket valve motor clocked 102.87mph and the racing eight-valve did 111.98.

Through the tremendous hectic racing years of the early 'twenties, both dealer and privately entered motorcycles supplemented the factory teams by competing in events that the works teams missed.

Bill Minnick astride one of the racing Harley-Davidson combinations renowned in America during the 1920s

Eddie Brinck, a great dirt track star, and his Harley-Davidson ''Peashooter''. Note the shirt and tie of the 'protected' rider

2 Australia catches on

A contingent of American riders went to Australia for the 1925-26 season of track racing on the concrete Maroubra circuit at Sydney. They found however, that small track racing was on the upgrade and were able to put across the cornering style they had accomplished on their home circuits. Cecil Brown, who was later to race in England, was the first American to show the Australians how to broadside; he was a great attraction wherever he raced, but others who immediately jumped into popularity were Eddie Brinck and "Sprouts" Elder.

It was back in 1923 that Johnnie Hoskins started his motorcycle activities and later turned out to be one of the most remarkable personalities in speedway racing and one who, despite his 84 years is still going strong at Canterbury Speedway today. A wonderful man ... with a wonderful life.

Johnnie landed at Maitland on the Hunter River Valley from Sydney with hardly any cash; he was looking for a job. A fellow by the name of Fred Fountain had been the Secretary of the local Agricultural Show Society for the previous twenty years and he resigned his employment. The Society had had some hard times and was in debt to their local bankers to the tune of over £3,000. The vacant position was advertised and Johnnie Hoskins — a New Zealander by birth — in dire need of money, applied for the job. Delighted to be the successful applicant, he immediately got down to the organisation of his first Show. This energetic young man, overflowing with enthusiasm, was well-suited as the new Secretary, his mode of transport being an ancient single-speed British single-cylinder motorcycle, which required the run-and-jump method of starting.

Incidentally, these Shows at West Maitland were called Electric Light Carnivals and were held on Saturday evenings. Included in the programmes were, horse-trotting, cycle racing, athletic events and even goat racing!

A very keen member of the Hamilton Motor Cycle Club named Les Upfold, who was working and staying in Maitland at that time, attended one of these Carnivals and hit on the idea of motorcycle racing under the lights. What a unique attraction he thought and approached Johnnie Hoskins, who agreed whole-heartedly with the new idea.

It was then arranged that a party from the Hamilton Club would visit the Maitland Show Ground on the following Sunday morning for a try-out. This group of riders were; Les Upfold (Norton), George Ross (American), Andy Eyre (Harley combination), with Claude Rankin as passenger, Bill Cogan (Douglas) and Bill Crampton (Norton). Andy Eyre was handicapper and time-keeper.

Johnnie started off on his belt-driven Triumph, but Bill Crampton flashed past him on the back straight to complete lap one. Hoskins was a little frightened; it was his first and his last ride on a motorcycle — at least race-wise!

After several laps with the stop-watch clicking away, it was decided that the riders attend the Show-ground on the following Saturday evening to race under the lights. On this occasion they were accompanied by other members of the Hamilton M/C Club, the Newcastle Club and the Maitland Club.

Johnnie Hoskins was a beaver for work and a genius in organisation and finally persuaded the Show Committee to promote motorcycle racing. The first meeting was held on December 15, 1923. The machines which faced the starter — the burly Jim Cameron — were a motley collection of ironmongery and, of course, the models were ridden to and from the track, a practice which was to continue for several years. The machines included; old Harley-Davidsons, Indians, Excelsiors, Douglases, BSAs and Triumphs. Also included in the programme was cycle racing, pole vaulting, horse trotting, the last appearance of Tom Handley's famous horse buck-jumpers and the Kurri Kurri Town Band.

Johnnie Hoskins, the most famous speedway promoter of all time on the right. This recent picture shows him with his wife Audrey and his son Ian

The new sport spread like a bush fire in country areas. People also came from the larger nearby towns of Cessnock, Newcastle, Singleton and Muswellbrook, to see the fun, which appealed to the young and old alike, who were thrilled by open exhausts, close racing, and the smell of Castrol R.

The Show Society was delighted with the efforts of the hard-working Hoskins and after a period of eighteen months that big bank debt had been repaid and the Committee wisely decided to make the track a banked one, provide cinders for the surface, and to construct a safety-fence. The latter however, was a necessity owing to spectator injuries after a 10hp Harley ran off the track.

Riding methods up to that point had been evolved to no set of rules, but the advent of the cinders — providing a loose surface — made new methods possible, and the first time that Billy Lamont, mounted on a potent AJS started to pour power into his rear wheel and to slide the bends in one controlled drift, quite a sensation was caused, as this method showed a clean pair of heels to the opposition.

Some of those original riders included: Arthur Aggett (Douglas), Roy Hindle (Chater Lea Blackburne), George Kirkwood (AJS), Les Petersen and Ernie Buck (Douglases), "Woppy" Bell (American Excelsior), Howard Moore (Ricardo Triumph), and many others astride Indian Scouts and Harley-Davidsons.

Jim Cameron, the race starter at Maitland was a wonderful enthusiast. With pipe in mouth he was known to everyone in Maitland as he rode to and from work on his massive Harley outfit. Besides being the local agent for BSA and Harley motorcycles he had been in his younger days a champion cyclist.

Motorcycle track racing in the Hunter River Valley actually dated back to 1909 when those case-hardened pioneers fought their ancient, high-framed, belt-driven castor oil-belching monsters around a quarter-mile slightly banked asphalt track, just off Porcher Street in Newcastle. Amongst the early riders were Cecil de Fraga, Jack Yee, Jim Lynch, Arthur Shephard and Ted McGee. Other well-known names that were added before the track closed in 1917 were Jack Turner, Bill Thomas, Charlie Wilson and Spindley Burnage.

In 1917 however, grass track racing was indulged in on the Newcastle Show Ground and during the following year, Sydney and interstate riders turned up to do battle with the locals on the one mile race-course at Wallsend, which was covered with long grass. Some new names included in the programme were Harry Krempin, Bill Turner, Mo Jones, Jack Rennie, Jack Hewson, Tommy Benstead and Arthur and Frank Mellor.

Other race tracks used on occasions from then on until 1924 were Rutherford, Dungog and Muswellbrook. 1924 saw the real birth of speedway racing as we know it today, the sport that was to thrill millions all over the world.

After Johnnie Hoskin's successful effort at Maitland Speedway, short tracks were quickly opened up at Cessnock and Singleton. Then in 1925 a Newcastle company constructed and opened the world's fastest half-mile track at Hamilton South with the ever-popular Johnnie as manager. It was a beautifully floodlit circuit of smooth red cinders and banked to the extent of six feet on the corners and three on the straights! The whole course of racing could be easily followed, yet 67 miles per hour was the usual average speed, and broadsiding at that speed was a terrifying spectacle!

It was here at Newcastle that Charlie Datson cracked Cecil Brown's two-mile record. Then a £50 prize was offered to anyone who could beat it with a 500cc machine. "Cess" clocked 1min., 55secs., and then Charlie bettered this by nearly 3 seconds. That same evening however, Datson broke the three-mile record and collected, in all, £150. His two-mile record stood for several years, although Pat Hamilton and Paddy Dean subsequently clocked two seconds less on 600cc Douglases.

The late Paddy Dean who covered a certified lap at Claremont Speedway at 72mph on a Douglas in 1926!

Charlie Datson flashes round the half-mile Claremont circuit near Perth on his Harley "Peashooter" in 1926.

44,000 enthusiasts attended the first meeting at Newcastle on November 14, 1925. Many world's records were toppled here, and some names to be remembered are the Americans Cecil Brown and Eddie Brinck; the New Zealanders, Spencer Stratton and Stewie St.George; the Sydney riders, Conaulty, Clifton and Benstead. Among the local riders who thrilled the public were; Billy Lamont, Jim and Charlie Datson, Billy Galloway, Ernie Buck, Irvine Jones, Paddy Dean, "Cowboy" Mills, Roy Hindle and scores of others. For a great number of years, Newcastle was considered the world's finest dirt track. Usually the dirt track programmes were made up with a big handicap event comprising up to 18 heats, 3 semi-finals, and a final. Considering that £4 18s was a good adult weekly wage in Australia at that particular time, the prize money was exceptionally good. First-place riders received £60, second-placed £20 and third-placed £10.

At the fabulous Newcastle circuit, Billy Lamont was certainly the thrill-maker with his 3½hp AJS, as also was Cecil Brown with his big Indians. And so was Stewie St.George and Jack Sweeney on their varied mounts, not forgetting the great Paddy Dean (Douglas) and Spencer Stratton on his Indian.

The dirt track sport grew with new circuits opening up. If Johnnie Hoskins was still to attract the top riders at his track, then he could plainly see that prize money would have to be increased. He fell on the idea of paying appearance money, and Cecil Brown, Spencer Stratton and Harry Peal were the first three riders in Australia to receive this type of incentive. All three were, of course, renowned for their performances on the giant concrete Maroubra track which allowed speeds of over 100mph, and the trio's appearance at Newcastle netted a sum of a thousand pounds.

The American Cecil Brown was undoubtedly one of the biggest draw cards in the sport. On one occasion Hoskins paid him £50 in appearance money, and arranged a Match Race with Charlie Datson. First Prize was £50 and the loser would get £25. Cecil won over £100 that particular evening, but his appearance made the gate receipts £400 above the average.

There was excellent racing too at the Deagon track — a mile in circumference — situated about 14 miles out of Brisbane. Everyone was greatly impressed with Deagon by the speed at which the top riders negotiated the wide, smooth curves and feet-up too. It was a sign of a serious lack of skill for a rider at that time to allow his foot to touch the ground, even under the most unfavourable circumstances!

Johnnie Hoskins transferred his activities to the Speedway Royale (third of a mile track) at Sydney in early 1926 and subsequently to Claremont Speedway near Perth. Billy Lamont, who later became an idol of the English fans, lapped at 67mph, while Paddy Dean, who also came to England, did a certified lap on a 750cc Douglas at 72mph. Really fantastic speeds when you consider they were being clocked fifty years ago!

Charlie and Jimmy Datson were the first riders to use Douglas machines for Australian dirt track racing, and Charlie's original motor was later housed in a museum at the Douglas works in Bristol, England, which has long since been disbanded. Sadly, both died of heart attacks in 1968.

Among the many riders Johnnie Hoskins recruited for the Sydney track was Eddie Brinck, who as I have already mentioned, was an American who had been a famous dirt tracker on the big circuits in the States and knew all that was to be known about speedway racing. He too, was a great showman, and whenever Johnnie put him in a programme, a packed stadium was a certainty. But Eddie knew his value, and also appreciated that infrequent appearances was the way to maintain it. Consequently he would not race more than once every three weeks at the Speedway Royale, and then only after Johnnie had put £50 in his hand!

Handicap races were extremely popular, but Eddie Brinck, a factory rider for Harley-Davidson, didn't like them. "Why should I take the risks of riding through a field of less competent riders?" he would ask, reasonably enough. He was very much afraid of someone falling off in front of him.

Eventually Eddie returned to his native country and what he had always feared, happened. He was involved in a terrible pile-up and, sad to relate, he was killed. This was while he was racing on a board track at Springfield, Mass., in August, 1927. Yes, everyone loved Eddie Brink, a showman supreme, and one of the greatest-ever riders. But now, unfortunately, he had ridden his last race.

Circuits at Adelaide and Penrith had now sprung up. Penrith Speedway, 30 miles from Sydney, was a remarkable track; nearly circular it gave a lap of one mile! Billy Connoulty lapped on a Douglas at an incredible 83mph, and this was in 1926. And in this same year, it was at the Newcastle Speedway that the half-mile dirt track Championship of Australia was staged in October, when a crowd of 25,000 watched Douglas machines sweep the board. All four riders, Hamilton, Sharp, Rees and McIntosh in the Final were mounted on 494cc TT Douglases. Hamilton finished first to win the £150 prize, and his time of 1min., 50 2/5 secs., was claimed as a world record for half-mile circuits. The other attraction of the meeting was a 4-lap Handicap Race for £75 prize money, which resulted in a Final win for Ernie Buck, also Douglas mounted.

The Australians tracks were, of course, very large circuits, conducive to exceptionally high speeds, and when A.J. Hunting started a quarter-mile track (the first of its kind) at the Brisbane Exhibition Grounds, many failed to see why anyone should care to go and watch what would possibly be a feeble imitation of the real thing. The speeds that enthusiasts had been used to, they argued, would be impossible on the tiny Exhibition circuit. They asked: "Where, then could be its attraction?"

But it certainly proved an attraction — a great attraction, and in that 1926-27 season, crowds of around the 30,000 mark regularly flocked to see what was hailed as a new form of motorcycle sport — and these came from a city of only 250,000! On one occasion Cecil Brown arrived in the pits with a knee-hook on the offside of his machine. To the natural enquiries as to the use of this particular item, he replied politely: "Ah, you better watch." The enthusiasts watched, and saw "Cess" deliberately trailing his left foot on the bends, and the riders, an enterprising band, were over-critical when they realised how very helpful the trailing leg could be.

However, the officials regarded Cecil's invention as a device which should be eradicated immediately, and there came a warning that any rider footing on a bend would be instantly disqualified.

The extraordinary sight of a group of officials on their hands and knees in order to see that no rider, and in particular Cecil Brown, transgressed this rule was something to be seen to be believed! Shortly after, the style of riding changed and the inside foot-rest was discarded.

This was not, however, as we were later to understand the term, dirt track racing. A.J. Hunting's circuit was a grass-track that had been used for trotting races. Nevertheless some of these early riders executed real broadsides with amazing steadiness. Charlie Spinks and Frank Pearce were the unquestioned stars. They had been champions on the grass, and now aided by suitable equipment and a natural aptitude for the new technique they were practicably unbeatable.

At this time there were several unknowns, including the names of Vic Huxley, Frank Arthur and Dicky Smythe, who hung enviously over the pit fence to watch the champions gaining their victories.

Let's take a deeper look at that first-ever Brisbane meeting, on October 16, 1926. The honour of winning the first race was gained by Vic Huxley, then a raw novice riding a stripped-down AJS roadster. Two subsequent races were won by other famous names-to-be in the speedway world, Frank Pearce and Frank Arthur. Pearce a wonderful grass-track exponent, had established a big reputation on 350cc machines, which he subsequently enhanced in speedway. To be spectacular never appealed to him, which was probably the reason why he was so successful. He seldom had trouble with his machines, in direct contrast to his unfortunate experiences later in England.

Frank, a Douglas and Harley Peashooter rider, was particularly anxious to win the first scratch race, for the Veedol Golden Helmet. Rain, late in the afternoon, made the track of unadulterated grass very slippery, so he decided to ride his longer wheel-based Douglas which proved a wise move as he gained a comfortable victory from Charlie Spinks in the Helmet Final.

The late Dicky Smythe was another rider who gained a host of speedway honours, and he won the 2-mile handicap Final. Several types of roadsters were being tried out, and these included — BSA, New Imperial, AJS, Levis, Scott, Indian and Harley.

The incomparable "Sprouts" Elder acknowledged as speedway's greatest showman

Brisbane's Exhibition Speedway flourished ... and flourished. A stereotyped programme of scratch races, handicaps and match races was the rule, as the distances between the various cities were so great that inter-track competitions were absolutely out of the question.

Incidentally, an Englishman was working as a mechanic in Brisbane at this time. His name was Arthur Yensen and he was a spectacular rider on an adapted AJS, but an appalling crash with Pearce and Spinks on the Harleys unfortunately ended his career as a first-rater.

Charlie Spinks, "Dare-Devil Charlie" they used to call him, was a great favourite with the enthusiasts in the early Exhibition days. Hence his nickname. Hence, too, his tremendous popularity — and his crashes. He had won a 100-mile track race at Toowoomba as far back as 1923 when he first started racing, and he won the main event at Brisbane's second, third and fourth meetings.

Announcements were made by a stentorian announcer, armed with a three-horned megaphone, who walked to the four corners of the circuit to announce the winners.

The late Frank Arthur (he died in 1972) failed to do big things at the Exhibition track. He was attached to a motorcycle agent firm and had to ride a heavy and very unsuitable machine. He tried extremely hard but, handicapped as he was, he generally finished up wrapped round some portion of the fence, or prostrate on a stretcher! A year later however, Frank severed his connection with the company, acquired the machine he most desired, and then went on to petrify spectators and opponents alike by a sudden transformation of riding abilities!

Vic Huxley, a very spectacular rider indeed, paid undeviating attention to the white line, and was very rarely in trouble. When he procured a good machine he was nigh invincible; this was on a Harley Peashooter. But Vic's methods were a little severe on frames. The lightly-built Harleys, originally designed for grass track racing, were never long in their correct alignment when he was in the saddle. The unusual amount of whip induced, often led to him losing a chain, and a race, when victory was in sight.

Equipment in those far off days was very meagre. Admittedly a crash helmet was worn, but a pair of leggings over ordinary work pants with a jersey on the top was the usual order. Needless to say, crashes were costly in skin and bruises but this type of sport could not be separated from them!

And so that initial Australian season drew to a triumphant end, but not before A.J.Hunting had come to the conclusion that even better racing would be forthcoming from a track specially designed and constructed for this new type of sport. Thus, speedway racing moved across the Brisbane River to Davies Park, where the first quarter-mile circuit to be designed expressly for dirt track racing was laid down for the ambitious Hunting.

This decomposed granite track with overhead lighting did not accommodate such crowds as did the Exhibition track with its stands and terraced seats, but it put the finishing touches to the technique of the novices, who mainly comprised the original competitors of 1926, and from Davies Park set forth the contingent of Australians who, in 1928, brought the sport to England.

Davies Park Speedway was a beautiful track. It was dead flat, and approximately the shape of a penny with the date cut off, that is to say, round except for one short straight. Its initial meeting took place in October, 1927, and Vic Huxley (Douglas) was the star performer, winning the Veedol Golden Helmet and the Royal Pennant events. It was here that Frank Arthur really came into his own. He won three Golden Helmet races in succession on a 500cc AJS, in a dirt track frame. Other Davies Park highlights included Charlie Spink's machine flying over the safety fence into the crowd — probably the first accident of this nature in speedway racing, and the appearance of the Townsville Champion, Max Grosskreutz.

A glorious shot of Billy Lamont who clocked up incredible successes on his high-framed AJS both in Australia and in Britain

3 Dirt track racing comes to Britain

It was Lionel Wills, a most valued member for many years of today's Veteran Dirt Track Riders' Association; the Hon. Secretary of the first-ever Dirt Track Riders' Association in England in early 1928, and an exceptionally good friend to everyone connected with speedway racing, who in 1926 left Cambridge University and departed on a part holiday, part business trip to Australia on a 500cc Rudge Whitworth. It was certainly something of a very ambitious adventure.

On his arrival he spotted an announcement in a Sydney newspaper — Speedway Royale — next Saturday. 8 p.m. Speedway was a strange new word to him but he had the intuition that it was to do with motorcycles. When Saturday came round he rushed to pay his admission fee. From the stands he heard a roar; the old familiar, unique and peculiar tearing sound of the twin-cylinder machine. Two machines were hurtling straight at him at a terrific speed and, seemingly out of control, and for the first time in his life Lionel shut his eyes and waited for the crash ... the crash which did not come. Sure enough there were the riders, tearing down the straight and madly leaning over into the next corner. "Wait until the racing starts," came a voice from behind. It was, of course, just a short practice session!

Lionel had lost control of his limbs and was forced to sit down through sheer excitement. Charlie Datson was scratch man in the initial race, and when he got going the riders who had been practising looked like raw novices. So this was dirt track racing and the more of it the better.

The keen tourist had been accustomed to grass track racing in England and path racing at the Crystal Palace but this game was so much different. The Australian riders simply amazed the lanky, well-spoken Englishman; he became so enthusiastic about their exciting broadsiding ability and their incredible speeds that he wrote to the British motorcycling press, enclosing cuttings, pictures and programmes which described this brand new sport, which he thought should certainly be introduced to Britain.

Not content with being a mere spectator, Lionel Wills was keen on having a go himself and, having found Sydney's Speedway manager, Johnnie Hoskins, high up on the tenth floor of a fantastic Sydney skyscraper, applied for a trial. And this on his sports Rudge roadster! Johnnie gave him a ride alright and although he rode his touring model really well, broadsiding proved much harder than it had looked.

Lionel's letters to the press had been given a good reception and on the strength of these reports, plus some very bold and enthusiastic spirits in the Camberley Club here in England, Club members staged on May 7, 1927 a very gallant attempt at a broadsiding display on Camberley Heath, billed and reported as Britain's First Dirt-Track Meeting. But it was nothing like a proper dirt track meeting, for the course was rough and consisted of sand which was too loose and deep and competitors rode the circuit the wrong way round — clockwise!

Albeit, it was a great attempt to put into practice what had appeared in print, even if it wasn't quite the real thing. But, nevertheless, no history of British speedway racing could ignore the fact that the Camberley event was the beginning. For the record however, C. Harman, riding a 349cc JAP engined OK Supreme not only gained the 350 Trophy but the 500 Trophy as well, and then with a sidecar attached went on to win the Sidecar Trophy!

Australian dirt track racing had enthused Lionel Wills to an extremely high degree. His fantastic and unbounded enthusiasm for the sport will forever be remembered by those who were fortunate enough to know one of the game's greatest sportsman and to enjoy his immensely likeable company.

Incidentally, Lionel Wills was the first-ever Englishman to become a dirt track rider. His sportsmanship was highlighted by the fact that he would never accept any prize money; it was highlighted too on one occasion at

Sydney Speedway. "Sprouts" Elder, after two crashes, was stuck for a motor and so Lionel loaned him his new machine, a Rudge. The American immediately accepted the kind offer, and then in a third spill, "Sprouts" smashed it to smithereens!

Lionel retired from business in 1960, and went to Trieste in Italy to reside. To the dismay of his countless friends and admirers he died seven years later. But back to his Australian tour. Whilst he was "sowing the good seed" another Englishman, and one who was destined to be closely associated with dirt track racing in England (a promoter too) came into the limelight. It was Stanley Glanfield who had in July, 1927 started an attempt on a Rudge Whitworth combination to encircle the world in 120 days! He landed in Australia at Port Darwin, on the Northern coast, and claimed to be the first-ever motorcyclist to accomplish the journey alone from that point to Sydney, a distance of 3,700 miles.

Incidentally, since 1930, Glanfield's historic machine was on display in the Kensington Science Museum in London. In July, 1967, the famous Round-the-World Rudge went on show at each of the various Glanfield-Lawrence motorcycle branches throughout Britain.

On arriving at Brisbane, Stanley Glanfield would not believe what they told him about two-wheelers sliding on a loose-surfaced track, and he was enticed to a meeting to see for himself, after which he immediately wrote home to say that he was sure a similar spectacle in England would attract regular crowds of 50,000. And how right he was later proved to be.

Glanfield arrived back in this country in December, 1927 after covering 23,000 miles. He later equipped the first workshops in the country devoted exclusively to the maintenance of speedway machines. This was at his Tottenham Court Road premises, in London.

Whilst in Australia, Glanfield discussed the possibilities of introducing dirt track racing to Britain, with various promoters, and the outcome was that A.J.Hunting, famous for his promoting capabilities, was determined to bring a contingent of Australian riders to England.

In the meantime several motorcycle clubs in England were toying with the idea of staging a dirt track meeting during the winter of 1927-28, but the only drawback seemed to be the big expense entailed in laying a track and a top question was: would the sport take on in Britain as it had in Australia?

Before anything definite had been arranged, Lionel Wills had landed in England. This was at Christmas, 1927, and, still bubbling over with dirt track enthusiasm, set about the task of getting his favourite sport on the move. He contacted Fred Mockford and Cecil Smith — promoters of the Crystal Palace's "path" racing — and also Jack Hill-Bailey, Secretary of the Ilford Motorcycle Club.

Lionel told them of dirt track racing and its wonderful thrills, broadsiding at high speeds round quarter mile and third of a mile tracks, and hair-raising stories of Paddy Dean, Billy Lamont, "Sprouts" Elder and others.

The construction of a brand new track needed, of course, an expert's advice and these were 12,000 miles away in Australia. It was agreed that one would certainly have to be sent for and naturally Lionel suggested Johnnie Hoskins. And so a cable went to Johnnie asking him to come to England as soon as possible.

As the Australian 1927-28 season came to a successful end, the late A.J'Hunting (he died suddenly while on a visit to Melbourne in 1946) decided to come to England with his band of pioneer riders which included such notable names as Frank Arthur, Vic Huxley, Charlie Spinks, Frank Pearce, Ben Unwin, Noel Johnson, Jack Bishop, Hilary Buchanan, Dicky Smythe, Billy Lamont and Cecil Brown. They came to England on the SS Oronsay — now lying at the bottom of the sea — and with them was the ever-faithful Johnnie Hoskins with his great trio — Ron Johnson, Charlie Datson and Sig Schlam who would, on landing, be heading for the Crystal Palace.

Meanwhile, Jack Hill-Bailey had long talks with Lionel Wills and the two Australians, Keith McKay and Geoff Meredith, who had arrived in England in October (1927) with the direct intention of promoting dirt track meetings.

The prominent Ilford Club secretary used his brains very hard. Where could a meeting be held in or near London? Jack's first inspiration was a half mile trotting track near his Ilford home. And so he approached his Club's President, the late Sir Frederick Wise, Ilford MP, who interviewed the London County Council, the owners of the track, and opened negotiations on the Club's behalf.

But suddenly a calamity happened, not only to the Club but to the whole of Ilford itself. Sir Frederick Wise died. Later Lady Wise told Hill-Bailey that her husband was still endeavouring to obtain the Parsloes trotting track right up to the time of his much-mourned death. Sir Frederick Wise was a wonderful personality, whose aid no one sought in vain.

Charlie "Ginger" Pashley broadsides his Sunbeam. He won the Trophy at Britain's first dirt track meeting at Droylesden, Manchester on June 25 1927

This reverse for the enterprising Ilford Club slowed things down a little ... but all was not lost. In searching for a suitable track, Hill-Bailey discovered the disused cycle track at King's Oak in Epping Forest and immediately negotiated for its use. The circuit was in the grounds of the King's Oak Hotel, at its rear, and Louis Marden, the proprietor, was all in favour of the idea. "Let the boys have their fun" he said. But even now the outlook was not all that rosy. For instance, the Ilford Club funds stood at a mere £30 and some members regarded the experiment as a super gamble. Indeed, rain on the all-important day would probably create a big row in the Club.

However the Secretary applied for a Sunday permit to the Auto-Cycle Union to hold a meeting in November, 1927. But the ACU would not grant an Open Permit for racing on the Sabbath and so the next best thing was to seek a Closed or Restricted Permit.

Incidentally, when it became known that the Ilford Club's original plans for that November meeting had fallen through, Hill-Bailey had considerable difficulty in keeping the riders from taking the law into their own hands and running the meeting, permit or no permit!

However Jack made a further application to the Eastern Centre Board of the ACU for a Restricted Permit for Sunday, February 19, (1928) restricted to the Ilford and Colchester Clubs, and it was granted.

The ACU sent three supervisory Stewards to inspect the King's Oak track. This was on a snowy day in January, when Jack Hill-Bailey discussed his plans with them. After some three hours the Stewards decided to recommend that provided certain requirements were carried out, the ACU would give its approval.

As the good news was broadcast, Hill-Bailey, a highly delighted fellow, received applications for Club membership from all the noted grass track and trials riders.

"With my wonderful wife's assistance", quoting his own words, Jack and his wife were writing letters to the tune of a hundred a night, and retiring to bed at two o'clock in the morning! In one case Jack had to go to the main Post Office as the small wall pillar box close to his home would not take his mail.

Entries came in thick and fast from such notables as; Colin Watson, Alf Foulds, Reg Pointer, Jack Barnett, Alf Medcalf, and Ivor Creek, with sidecar drivers, Noterman, Pellat and Gordon Norchi — names that would draw a crowd anywhere.

A group of Australian speedway pioneers who landed in England in early 1928. From left to right; *Vic Huxley, Buzz Hibberd, Frank Arthur, Max Grosskreutz, Billy Lamont and seated, Hilary Buchanan*

At the first ever meeting at King's Oak (February 19 1928) Billy Galloway shows the first steel toe-cap to the Press, on the foot of Keith McKay

And so the great day came round. February 19, 1928. The time: 7.30 a.m. The weather: fine and sunny.

An olive green Harley-Davidson combination of 11 hp and one that had competed in 'Open' long-distance reliability trials, such as the London-Gloucester-London the year before, is wheeled from its garage in Hickling Road, Ilford. A sharp kick on the starter and the twin-cylinder machine's lusty bark echoes up the street. Jack Hill-Bailey mounts his massive outfit; his wife Kay sits in the sidecar with 2,000 tickets and 500 programmes on her lap. Into first gear and away they roar in the direction of Epping Forest, some ten miles away, for here tucked away serenely in its heart is the King's Oak track and real dirt track racing is about to blast forth in fantastic style.

At this point I should add, as a stickler for literal facts, that this King's Oak meet was not actually Britain's first-ever dirt track meeting, although it is generally acknowledged as such.

If you believe that cinder-track racing is the true definition of dirt track racing — as most of us do — and that the Camberley Club's sand meeting — mentioned previously — is not strictly in the dirt track category, then the South Manchester Motor Club holds the honour of staging the first-ever dirt track meeting in Britain. This was at Dodds Farm, Droylesden, on the outskirts of Manchester on June 25, 1927, for which an ACU permit was issued. The circuit, a trotting track, which was a third-of-a-mile round, had banked bends, and was composed of hard cinders.

One of the stars of the day was the sandy-haired genial Charlie Pashley, a rider destined to be an ace in midget-car speedway racing. Riding his Sunbeam he won the 600cc 3-lap experts event and clocked the fastest time of day for which he received the Trophy, in front of about a thousand spectators. Fred Fearnley, who was to turn up again in speedway later on at West Ham, won the 200cc 3-lap event on his little 172cc Francis-Barnett. He also came second in the 200cc 10-lap event, and after attaching a sidecar to it, took second place in the 350cc event. Riding a Rudge outfit he was again second in the sidecar unlimited. Another star of the day was Ronald Cave, riding a Cotton. He gained victories in the 350cc 10-lap event and the 600cc 3-lap Novice Event.

Incidentally, Charlie "Ginger" Pashley, one of the first members of the Belle Vue Aces and later skipper of the Belle Vue midget car racing team, died at his home in Cheadle in March, 1973.

But to return to the King's Oak circuit on February 19, 1928, situated at High Beech, a rural precinct

The car park at King's Oak. Scenes like this became familiar as dirt track racing caught on

consisting mainly of the imposing King's Oak Hotel and its assorted out-buildings. Jack Hill-Bailey and his wife duly arrive at 8 am. Already there is a large crowd gathered round the Hotel even though the show does not start for another two and a half hours. The tickets and the 500 programmes are unloaded at the track's entrance. Boxes are made up as a desk to serve the cash customers. Admission is sixpence (2½p).

An entry list of 42 riders will compete in eight main events consisting of fifty-odd races.

And what a day! It should have been the middle of June, not February, with brilliant sunshine such as this. Jack Hill-Bailey, founder of the Ilford Club, rounds up the Steward and other officials; it is 9.30 am and all the tickets have been sold and every programme too; the barriers have all been pushed over; the barbed wire fence surrounding the ground has been completely cut down as well as the entrance gate, and all hope of collecting further admission fees has vanished!

Incidentally, Jack's committee had previously decided that if 3,000 people turned up, the Club would have done extremely well, especially in view of the fact that snow had been falling in that area some days previous.

It is 10 am and from 12,000 to 15,000 people are inside the arena and many thousands are still along the approach roads. Every police station in a radius of ten miles is 'phoned for reinforcements; the road traffic is blocked on all sides and the roads throughout the east of London.

Jack Hill-Bailey is, not surprisingly, looking a happy but somewhat dazed man. Even an hour later the King's Oak approaches from both directions are choked with traffic, mainly motorcycles. Still later, as the crowd swells relentlessly through, 16,000, 20,000 and on to an estimated 30,000, the poor harassed Secretary, haunted by the chaotic conditions, is assuming the hunted look of a very worried fellow!

The ACU had insisted that all spectators were to be kept behind the rope barrier INSIDE the track! It is obvious to everyone that this rule could not be obeyed and the multitude is swarming, like bees in a nest, around the outside of the course.

The beech trees standing back from the track perimeter, provide multi-storey perching and many view the proceedings from a crow's-nest angle. Wal Phillips — destined to become one of Britain's greatest riders — is one!

The ball was set rolling with a 5-lap Novice event consisting of six heats with three riders in each, two semi-finals, and a final, the latter being won by Fred Ralph on a Coventry-Eagle.

Fred Ralph (no 21) riding a Coventry Eagle leads Ivor Creek on a Norton in a solo event at King's Oak, High Beech's first meeting

When the 5-lap solo and the 5-lap sidecar events had been completed there came the lunch interval, after which AA officials computed the value of cars, motorcycles, etc., in the forest area outside the dirt track to value £1,500,000 sterling, and a total crowd of thirty-thousand! To obtain refreshments had been an almost impossibility, and Jack Hill-Bailey had evidence that in spite of several inns and hotels in the vicinity, some folk travelled five miles to obtain sandwiches and drinks!

Knowing very little as yet, of what true dirt track racing was like, everyone thought the racing was absolutely hell on wheels, but in later months, in retrospect, the enthusiasts realised that what they had been witnessing was a pack of novices — except Billy Galloway and Keith McKay — who nevertheless, performed in an exceptionally courageous and determined way. The machines used were a mixed bag of roadster and grass track types — Sunbeams, Ariels, AJS's, OK — Supremes, Douglases and all the rest.

Under an ACU ruling every machine had to be fitted with brakes which were, in some circumstances, used often and violently. But not in the case of Galloway and McKay, Jack Hill-Bailey's star men, the two veritable Australians, exponents of the art of broadsiding.

If the impending visit of these two renowned riders, all the way from New South Wales, had been advertised it might well have had the effect of doubling the attendance to perhaps 60,000! But lacking the financial resources to go in for a big advertising campaign, and little dreaming that the appeal of the event would probably not extend beyond East London and inner Essex, the Ilford Club's preliminary announcements were very meagre.

To compete in the meeting, the two Australians joined the 1,000 strong Metropolis Motor Club headed by Jimmy Baxter and the word Metropolis was boldly written across the front of their leathers.

Incidentally, Keith McKay was later involved in a bad crash at Sydney Speedway in the Australian 1929-30 season, breaking his leg in several places and receiving other injuries from which, sad to say, he died.

The first big spectator thrill came in heat 3 of event two. Billy Galloway (494cc Douglas) owing to a bad start was last on lap one; cutting out for a second as he entered the one and only loose bend, he opened the throttle full, to be rewarded not by a broadside but a series of vicious, spectacular skids. Continuing in this style, he wriggled through the field, finally passing Colin Watson (346cc New Imperial) ... the same Colin who was destined to beat the best and bring the crowds to their feet right up until July 13, 1946, when a serious crash at Odsal put him out of the sport that he loved and had served so gallantly for so long.

The hard cinder track at King's Oak was unsuitable for sliding. The two Australians had, of course, been used to a continuous loose surface, but Galloway and McKay were doing their best. The real dirt track Duggies were yet to come and the Douglas that Billy was riding was actually Freddie Dixon's Isle of Man TT machine with road-race gearing! And he never got out of bottom gear. Keith was provided with — by the Douglas company — a hotted-up 2¾hp Douglas to ride, but it wouldn't pull the skin off a rice-pudding. With the crowd in such precarious positions it was probably just as well!

Billy Galloway had been working as a hairdresser in Holborn (London) after previously being employed in the same capacity on the Oronsay, the ship that brought him from Australia and had landed him at Tilbury at Christmas, 1927. Even today Bill describes this first-ever King's Oak meet as "the most exciting dirt track meeting in my life, with people outside and inside the track who had to draw in their stomachs to let you get around the white line."

After gaining second place to Alf Foulds (Sunbeam) in the semi-final Solo event, Billy Galloway then came up against Reg Pointer (Ariel) in the Final, a race which made even the most staid spectators gasp and women scream. Reg started off well but found himself going wide; he suddenly braked and cut in on Billy, which was something that an expert dirt tracker did not expect. The Australian's Duggie reared up and threw him off, and although uninjured, he had strained his neck.

But Billy Galloway had made a grand British debut. A photographer had captured his spectacular spill, and it made the news and the picture for the next day's papers.

The sidecar racing provided great interest especially as they raced anticlockwise, the same as the solos. The driver's passenger was always working overtime in valiant efforts to keep the sidecar wheel on the ground! C.M.Harley, 488cc Zenith sidecar, won the first sidecar event and A.Noterman (Triumph) the second.

Among the solos, the English star rider, both as regards time and as a spectacle, was Alf Medcalf of the Colchester Club. He lapped on a 348cc Douglas in 26.8secs., and machine-wise he was the best equipped. Comparing his Duggie with its low weight, flexible frame and the cinder-slicing torque for which Douglases were famous, massive roadsters, like Ivor Creek's camshaft Norton, looked very much out of place.

During the meeting, the famous Australian promoter, A.J.Hunting, who had arrived in England that morning, turned up. He viewed the proceedings with a critical eye and was somewhat dismayed. Finding his way through the crush and over to a very harassed Jack Hill-Bailey he exclaimed: "My boy, you're all wrong — this isn't the way to run a dirt track meeting!"

Jack fully knew it was all wrong. What right had 30,000 people to cram inside a ground which had accommodation for a mere 2,000? How could he have anticipated that multitude? How was he to know that it was going to be a summer's day in the middle of February? Of course it was all wrong!

It was not until hours later, when the vast crowd had disappeared, that Jack and other members of the Ilford Club, realised the true meaning of their success. "Right or wrong," he said to his Committee members, "we've certainly started the ball rolling and no-one knows where it will stop."

The programme finished without a single casualty to riders or spectators. "It was due to the wonderful ability of our riders" remarked Hill-Bailey. "Never in the history of racing had a meeting been run under such conditions. Our organisation was severely tested, but came through with flying colours; superhuman efforts were required, and no-one was found wanting."

That impressive first-ever King's Oak show was the spark that kindled the flame.

Incidentally, at one of King's Oak's later meetings, "Dicky" Bird — a regular AJS exponent — unfortunately swallowed a wasp when actually racing and had to be taken to hospital. Truly, a unique occurrence, as no such thing has ever happened in speedway since. Sadly, Leonard "Dicky" Bird died suddenly at his Woodford Bridge home in 1949, at the early age of forty.

Billy Galloway crashes behind an Ariel rider at King's Oak, and makes the next day's papers

Arthur Noterman (Triumph) wins the sidecar event. His passenger, Fred Mundy, still holds a medal for that success. Note how close the crowd is to the machine

4 Climbing on the band wagon

The Ilford Club sought A.J.Hunting's valuable advice; he re-designed the King's Oak circuit and made other suggestions as to vital improvements. It was arranged for an Easter meeting to be held and big financial assistance came from W.J.Cearns and F.D.Smith.

Envisaging a rapid growth of dirt track racing the Auto-Cycle Union saw that it was its clear duty, as the body that supervised all forms of motorcycle sport, to encourage and control it. This duty fell upon a newly-formed sub-committee, known as the Track Licensing Committee, which held its first meeting on February 24, (1928).

The major difficulties encountered by this new Committee were due to the fact that, unlike all the older forms of the sport, this new branch was promoted not so much by the Clubs as by individuals or groups of individuals formed into companies, with the avowed object of making vast profits out of dirt track racing. The Committee however, consisted of Major Vernon Brook, Major Potter, the Rev.E.P.Greenhill, A.J.M.Ivison and the Secretary of the Union.

In the face of considerable opposition and suspicion, the Track Licensing Committee worked extremely hard to get this new branch of the sport established on a sound basis, and their faith in its continued success and their labours were amply justified during the ensuing years.

As a result of the new Track Licensing Committee being instituted, the modified King's Oak circuit was inspected and approved for the Easter Monday meeting — a two-part affair.

While King's Oak was being knocked into shape things were moving fast in other directions. Frank Longman, destined to be the winner of the Isle of Man Lightweight TT race a few months ahead and to be so sadly killed in the same category event five years later, made plans with a bunch of enthusiasts to form the Greenford Motor Club, and to take over the half mile pony trotting track at Greenford in Middlesex. Their object too, was to open at Easter.

Keith McKay had journeyed North and contacted the South Manchester Motor Club. He set about making preparations at another trotting track at Audenshaw, to hold dirt track meetings.

Dirt track racing on a circuit similar to those used overseas had yet to be witnessed in this country; a loose surface on which broadsiding was easily developed was the characteristic of the Australian and American tracks, and Audenshaw wasn't quite like this, for its surface was typically the hard cinder variety, similar to that of King's Oak. But whether any more lurid riding would have been witnessed on a softer track by the 15,000 spectators in the enclosures, on the stands, and even on the roofs of the stands on March 3, was something of an unknown quantity.

As it was the thrills were there in plenty, but those who were anxious to learn if Australian broadsiding was faster than our own riders' method of riding the bends were disappointed, for the Australians Galloway and McKay were unable to demonstrate any advantage over the local boys.

With King's Oak sensational opening and Audenshaw attracting a big crowd, thousands were now dirt track conscious. Other venues were exploited all over the place. Plans were going ahead for tracks at Huddersfield, Blackpool, Glasgow, and at Edinburgh. There were others too.

The Greyhound Racing Association saw great possibilities in the new sport. If a thirty-thousand crowd could be attracted to a comparatively remote place such as King's Oak in the heart of Epping Forest, how many could be drawn to their big stadiums such as Stamford Bridge, Harringay and the White City?

In consultation with Johnnie Hoskins, plans were drawn up for the Crystal Palace track; it was to be a three-lap circuit, Australian fashion. But the ground was just too small, and rather than have it an odd size, an exact 440 yards lap was chosen.

In the past, Britain's great motorcycle sport had been free from any taint of underhand work; the average competition rider, no matter whether he was in the trade or riding purely for the fun of it, played the game, and in some instances going so far as to help an opponent in trouble.

All who had any knowledge of reliability trials and racing, as carried on in the country, knew this to be the case. Commercialisation and betting: that was what the Clubs were strongly against.

Many however, were convinced that dirt track racing conducted in a proper way would prove a great attraction to the public, but discredit upon the promoters, and the pastime as a whole, would have followed the congregation of unwieldy crowds at Sunday race meetings. And so the ban by the ACU came down on any proposed Sunday meeting. A no betting rule was also instigated.

Easter Monday came round and 17,000 spectators turned up to watch some spectacular riding on the newly-constructed King's Oak track. There were two meetings — one in the morning and one in the afternoon! Seventeen thousand attended the first and ten thousand the second. And they all had a high quota of thrills. The circuit was, thanks to Bill Cearns' financial help, a marvellous improvement on the one used on February 19, and, for the first time in the country real true broadsiding was witnessed. The man who provided it was Alf Medcalf (494cc Douglas) who won the 500cc Grand Prix, after a wonderful tussle with Gus Kuhn (Calthorpe). Jack Barnett, today's Secretary of the Veteran Riders' Dirt Track Association, came third on an Ariel.

For everyone, thanks to members of the Ilford Club and in particular to Secretary, Jack Hill-Bailey, it had been another wonderful day's sport and from now on there would be racing at King's Oak every Saturday afternoon. We all regretted the passing of Jack, aged 69, in late 1952. He was a constructional engineer in the LNER. During the war he went to Germany to take charge of an American marshalling yard, with such success that he was later awarded the British Empire Medal. Speedway was greatly in Jack's debt, and all of us had lost a jolly good friend.

The New Zealander, Stewart St. George, who showed the spectators what this broadsiding business was all about

The Australian ace Billy Galloway often gave spectacular exhibition rides on his Douglas, demonstrating the broadside technique, which became an integral part of his dirt track racing.

Over the years a great deal has been written about King's Oak dirt track in the history of speedway racing in this country, but those articles, being largely factual and documentary, cannot capture for me, the atmosphere of the place.

High Beech, situated in the heart of Epping Forest, between Waltham Abbey and Loughton in Essex, was not an easily accessible spot. But on Bank Holidays, thousands of enthusiasts from East London and surrounding districts would make the trip, either by train to Loughton Station, and then the long trek up to the top, or by 102 or 38 number buses, the service being extended from the Royal Forest Hotel at Chingford, for the day, right up to the King's Oak Hotel.

King's Oak, is for me, always associated with that holiday atmosphere, with fair-ground music, ice-cream and fruit vendors and hundreds of picnickers sitting on the grass or on fallen tree trunks, admiring the view across the Lea Valley towards the ancient church tower of the Abbey Church at Waltham.

Behind the imposing King's Oak public house, was the dirt track and, under the trees were cars and trucks with carriers and trailers bearing, Douglas, Harley-Davidson, Rudge, New Imperial, Cotton, Calthorpe, AJS, BSA or a Coventry-Eagle dirt track bike, ready to be unloaded and wheeled down beside the hotel to the pits.

On such occasions there was usually a morning and afternoon meeting, so it was a double-feature day! And all for one shilling (5p)!

By the time the roar of motorcycles warming-up assailed the ears, and the smell of dope in the nostrils, many lads would be high up in the branches of the trees that surrounded the circuit, and getting their racing free! Inside the track the holiday atmosphere also prevailed. One small stand for the 'sitters', the rest of the crowd standing on the grassy mounds outside the dark wooden safety fence. No lamp standards or dog-track posts to impede the view; a complete and uninterrupted view of the near-on circular circuit was possible.

Jack Hill-Bailey in flannels, a jazzy pullover and trilby hat, was at the starting line, marshalling the riders and seeing them off to the push or flying starts. Once away from the short straight, the riders, on a host of different makes of machine, had to put their bikes into a continual power-slide, right round the circuit, the continual curve of the D, which was the shape of the track.

Home riders like Syd Edmonds (the Chingford laundryman), Jack Barnett, (a Water Board employee) or Phil Bishop (from his father's cycle shop in Roman Road, Old Ford), were past-masters at the art. Jack was for a long while, quite invincible on the track and seemed to hold a permanent ownership of the Mason Trophy which was awarded, weekly, to the rider clocking the fastest time of day. But one day there came the Harley Peashooter of Colin Watson's and he 'cleaned the board' and, I believe, after that was given Star status, being able to have a red number on his bike instead of a black one.

I remember, as a very young schoolboy, one particular King's Oak meet, when the morning meeting was over, wandering around the pits armed with an autograph book, obtaining signatures of the riders and watching their preparations for the afternoon meeting. Fritz Niemick and Arnold Stolting, two young German riders, were being given some riding tips by Phil Bishop. The language barrier seemed rather a high one! They gladly signed my book, adding to their autographs a German greeting. Phil Bishop scrawled his name across the page in his typical carefree manner, while Jack Barnett signed in his very neat and stylish handwriting. The pages of that book were inscribed with the names of most of the well-known riders of the day. Highly-valued, I still have it today.

The afternoon meeting consisted of a match; the Foresters against the Lea Bridge Team. The Australian Harold Hastings was riding for The Bridge, along with Jimmy Stevens and Alf Foulds, the latter being amongst the very earliest of riders at King's Oak. I remember that Harold rode the Forest circuit with greater ease and skill than I had seen him ride his home track at Lea Bridge. I remember him too, at his first practise at Lea, when Vic Huxley was there giving him valuable advice.

And Lea Bridge went home the losers. We went home on the long trek to Loughton Station, simply longing for the next time when we could again go to High Beech. Come to think of it, I never did pay the admission dues for that afternoon meeting! I was milling, like all the other youngsters, around the paddock and when the afternoon session was about to begin, I was already in!

Greenford's half mile track opened for its initial meeting in early April, after King's Oak, but there was no broadsiding. In compensation however, the thrilling spectacle of riders dashing through sheets of flame and thick smoke was witnessed by the large crowd. It was A.Welston (346cc New Imperial) who hit the fence, his machine

Frank Arthur in action on his 350cc Harley "Peashooter" at London's White City track in 1928

Australia versus America, at the White City in 1928. Billy Lamont (AJS) left, and Art Pechar (Indian) just before a Match Race

Another Australian speedway pioneer, Frank Duckett. He later joined Dirt Track Speedways Limited

immediately bursting into flames. After this exciting start, out came the redoubtable Billy Galloway and his Duggie who proceeded to win the Ealing Trophy Race at no less than 47.62mph and the 5-lap Greenford Trophy Race.

A few Australian riders — the vanguard of the contingent that was to follow — arrived in England, among them being Stewie St.George, "Brisbane" Smith and "Digger" Pugh. The latter however, was engaged at the King's Oak circuit to initiate the novices into the art of sliding. On the Friday following Easter Monday a giant of a youngster turned up on a 499cc Rudge Whitworth. He stripped off its near-side footrest and one or two other incidentals, and proceeded to ride round the track which was nearly a complete circle in shape.

The youngster had never seen the track before, but after a little while he opened the taps and started to slide. It was not surprising that he fell off a number of times, but with great determination he pegged away and made faster times with every lap. His name? Roger Frogley, of course, a farmer's son who lived at Cherry Tree Farm, Hoddesdon, not very far away.

In the end Roger was beating tutor Pugh, who, in all fairness was severely handicapped by his poor little Dunelt two-stroke of only 249cc!

The next afternoon, Saturday, Roger with the same machine competed in the King's Oak meeting with great success. He really thrilled the crowd time and again and established two new records for the Epping Forest circuit besides winning the 5-lap 500cc event. It was, of course, without the slightest stretch of imagination, a magnificent performance.

But it was at Greenford on the same afternoon when the spectators had their first taste of the real thing. Even before the meeting started everyone was talking about a New Zealander, Stewie St.George, who had sent his entry by cable and had flown the last part of his journey. He came out on his 494cc Douglas and made everyone's hair stand on end. On Greenford's long straights and big bends he laid his Duggie over at impossible angles; it was a broadsiding exhibition that completely thrilled the enthusiasts.

Although wonderfully spectacular, Stewie's display was cut short for Alf Foulds, later a member of the Clapton Team, fell in front of the New Zealander and in avoiding his Sunbeam, injured his hand when he scraped the wire safety fence. Unfortunately he was not able to compete in the remainder of the programme, much to the disappointment of the watchers.

Of course, Billy Galloway was there too, and he also demonstrated the broadsiding capabilities of his Douglas. He won the London Cup Race for Grade A riders. But Les Blakeborough, a great English personality who was destined to join Stamford Bridge, was the most successful competitor. His 348cc Cotton took him to victories in the Brentford, Alperton and Hanwell Cup races.

Two of the greatest riders ever seen in speedway racing, "Sprouts" Elder and Vic Huxley (right)

A few days later, Stewie St.George (who died in 1946) went to the Bristol Douglas factory and consulted John Douglas. Machine improvements were discussed, with the result that the dirt track Douglas was built with a frame made up of the front section of the RA model and the back section of the OC model. This particular machine was later ridden by Stewie at the Manchester track and after the meeting, Douglas Motors received the following telegram from him: "Motor and frame perfect. Won everything — St.George." After this success the hybrid frame was adopted for all dirt track Douglases.

With two London tracks already thriving, it was not surprising to see the sport spread quickly to the provinces. April 21, (1928) saw Blackpool stepping into the picture with a specially-prepared half mile track at the South Shore, organised by the North Manchester Club. But the surface of the circuit consisted principally of sand which was packed too hard to give the necessary conditions for broadsiding. Eric Langton (346cc New Hudson) and his brother, Oliver (498cc Scott) plus "Ginger" Lees, were the outstanding performers. And "Ginger" incidentally, was one of the first riders to adopt successfully the foot-forward style of riding.

At last the acknowledged Australian cracks arrived. The Oronsay docked at Southampton. There was Johnnie Hoskins and his trio of West Australians, Sig Schlam, Charlie Datson and Ron Johnson, and A.J.Hunting's contingent — predominantly Queenslanders — including Frank Arthur, Frank Pearce, Charlie Spinks, Hilary Buchanan, Dicky Smythe, Ben Unwin, Noel Johnson (who, sad to say, met with a fatal accident on the Plymouth track late in 1932), Jack Bishop, and the never-to-be-forgotten American, "Sprouts" Elder. Billy Lamont and Cecil Brown travelled to England via America.

A.J.Hunting formed International Speedways Ltd. He was the Managing Director, who gave a luncheon at London's Savoy Hotel in May to welcome its Australian riders.

By now the ACU had completed its new Track Racing Regulations: No Sunday racing; no public betting; all riders to wear leather clothing, non-splinterable goggles and crash helmets. There would be only two types of starting: the rolling start and the standing start. Maximum engine capacities would be 500cc for solo machines and 600cc for sidecar machines. These were the chief points.

The rival company to International Speedways, under the astute management of Jimmy Baxter, was called Dirt Track Speedways Ltd. who obtained working arrangements with other Australians such as Paddy Dean, Irvine Jones, Billy Galloway, Keith McKay and Frank Duckett.

Under the direction of the DTS syndicate, Celtic Park Speedway at Glasgow opened on April 28. It was Scotland's first-ever meeting. There appeared the finest and most impressive group of riders yet seen: Elder, Dean, Galloway, Meredith, St.George and McKay. But Celtic Park was not a great success, the crowds being around the 5,000 mark. Expenses were very high and prize money totalled £400 per meeting, apart from appearance money and bonuses.

May 5, (1928) was a fantastic day for dirt track enthusiasts in London. Three meetings in one day! The Australian Champions had been billed to appear at King's Oak, but Billy Lamont was unable to appear. However, there was an able substitute in Vic Huxley and a crowd of 12,000 saw the genuine Australian ace in action for the first time, and what a thrill that was! His first feat was to break Roger Frogley's lap record with a new speed of 40.7mph, and afterwards to break his 5-lap record.

At Greenford that same afternoon, "Sprouts" Elder made his initial London appearance on his Douglas. The showman supreme gave a wonderful performance and really gave the crowd what they had come to see; an exhibition of broadsiding that eclipsed everything they had previously seen.

That same evening, a great crowd made the trip to Stamford Bridge, to see Britain's first floodlit speedway. The air became almost electric as Stewie St.George and "Sprouts" Elder came out for their exhibition rides. Firstly Stewie gave his demonstration, sweeping cinders straight over the safety fence into the crowd. Then "Sprouts" put in a perfect and even faster ride, with sparks flying from the underside of his engine as it ploughed through the cinders. What had appeared fast that afternoon at Greenford, looked almost terrifying under the lights. The narrow track, and the noise thrown back by the terraces, added to the tremendous excitement.

For a moment longer the crowd held its breath; then came the roar. Hats and programmes were flung into the air in a wild burst of enthusiasm. So this was real speedway racing! Let's have some more!

A true broadsider; the tall, gangling, tungsten-muscled "Sprouts" Elder, from Fresno, California, had come to Britain following a successful season in Australia.

This opening evening at Stamford Bridge was, of course, a great occasion. Thirty thousand spectators ... eleven spills ... two exhibitions of real cinder-shifting. Everything was a feature in London's first night of illuminated

It happens to every rider sooner or later! Dicky Bird (AJS) 'lays it down' at King's Oak

dirt track racing. The track spattered with the yellow haze of lights ... the coloured jackets of the riders ... the blobs of thousands of faces filling the old football grandstand to the highest tier ... officials in white coats and sashes ... the press box packed with London reporters from the dailies and evenings and, above all, the howling noise of machines roaring and echoing within a few miles of London's centre.

And so The Bridge, a fast, banked quarter mile circuit, began a great season which was to bring fame to many a rider and a fortune to those who had the courage to finance such an ambitious scheme. In that 40-meeting season Stamford Bridge drew a total gate of over half a million!

Soon after this milestone in speedway's history came another, for two weeks later, in the afternoon of May 19, Crystal Palace staged its first meeting under the watchful eyes of Johnnie Hoskins, Fred Mockford and Cecil Smith. The track — which became Britain's fastest quarter miler — cost £5,025 to construct. Unfortunately it rained ... and rained, and machine trouble was much in evidence.

In the evening, International Speedways Ltd. commenced its comparatively short, but glamorous career with a meeting at London's White City, after a thunderstorm. Nevertheless, Billy Lamont (Douglas), Vic Huxley (Douglas), Dicky Smythe (Douglas), Frank Arthur (Harley), Ben Unwin (AJS), Hilary Buchanan (AJS) and Frank Pearce (Harley), all proved they could put across "the real thing."

Now came a spate of track openings. Wimbledon a week later; Harringay the following day; and a host of provincials within the next few weeks. With three major tracks in operation (White City, Wimbledon and Harringay), International Speedway Ltd. — the promoters — put a number of competitions into force and competitions of high-sounding titles. They were The Golden Helmet, The Golden Gauntlet, The Silver Armlet, The Silver Sash, The Silver Helmet, The Silver Wheel and The Silver Wings. Each and every one resulted in the award of a beautifully-designed Trophy.

The method of scoring was that riders in heats received one point; riders in semi-finals three points and in the final the winner received thirteen points, second eleven, third nine and fourth seven. These points accumulated during the season, and the rider with the highest average was acclaimed the winner of that particular Trophy. There was also a special bonus accompanying the prize money. These competitions were also staged at other London circuits as they opened up.

The Halifax track had opened on May 2 with evening meetings on a hard narrow cinder track surrounding the Thrum Hall cricket ground, and the circuit was illuminated by acetylene flares!

The roar of open exhausts was first heard at the Marine Gardens, Portobello — the "seaside" of Edinburgh on May 19, and Jimmy Fraser was the man in charge. His death in 1941 robbed Scotland of an extremely popular manager. At Edinburgh's initial meetings bookmakers were reported to be unofficially operating, but this was soon stopped. The track, 440 yards, was open to the novices who kept struggling away. Then an apparition in a complete set of black leathers suddenly made his appearance. Australia had arrived in the person of Paddy Dean. Everyone thought he was mad. Of all the hair-brained dare-devils they considered Paddy the worst. Lap after lap he tore round the track, almost riding on his ear; how he kept his seat seemed a miracle and the law of gravitation seemed to have no meaning for him.

Acknowledged as Britain's first speedway champion, Roger Frogley is here on his 500cc Rudge-Whitworth roadster in 1928

The name of just one Australian in Edinburgh's first programme was sufficient to bring 20,000 enthusiasts to Portobello ... no one now wanted to see the locals perform!

Edinburgh welcomed dirt track racing with open arms, and it soon became a definite part of the sporting life of the capital of Scotland. Whereas many believed this new sport was no more than a passing craze; a few foresaw a big-time future for it.

With Lea Bridge and West Ham starting up in July, the total number of tracks in or on the outskirts of London crept to nine, and with Belle Vue joining the ranks of new circuits late in July, speedway racing could then be said to be truly established.

Tracks grew throughout the country like mushrooms and eventually some withered and died.

Barnsley had opened in May as well as Wolverhampton, followed by Brighton in June and Birmingham and Bradford in July. Then came Bristol, Huddersfield, Rochdale, Salford and Swindon in August and in the following month Coventry opened its gates. Southampton came in as late as October as also did Leeds, while Cardiff staged its first-ever dirt track meeting on December 26th!

International Speedways Ltd., were delighted with the attendances, and their contract riders were really in the money. If you were an International Boy you had anything from £100 to £320 a week virtually guaranteed to you. Many programme fillers drew the lesser sum regularly, while the real top-notchers such as Huxley and Arthur frequently touched the higher figure.

It was riders like the never-to-be-forgotten "Sprouts" Elder who made the dirt track Douglas and was acknowledged as speedway's greatest showman. He had the best and fastest models in the game. At Stamford Bridge for example, he charged a fee of £100, but if he was asked to ride in an additional race, the shrewd American received a further £25 or even more, so that he often took £150 away with him after an evening's work.

"Sprouts" once admitted that he made £350 in one day as the result of his speedway activities, by riding at three north-country tracks which were near to each other.

Lloyd Elder, his proper name, was unique amongst a bunch of truly remarkable riders. He was fearless, and his superb performances won him a warm place in the hearts of every dirt track enthusiast. First and foremost a showman, he was a wonderful asset in any programme in which he might appear with the more successful, but less hair-raising, Frank Arthur and Vic Huxley.

Tall, (six foot, three inches), thin, and with utter disregard for convention of any kind, the American ace created a sensation wherever he raced. Winning or losing he was always worth watching. This loose-limbed six-footer was a master of bluff and used it to the full in races whenever necessary. This humorous fellow, who broke all rules so joyfully — and for a period he even raced in an ordinary flying helmet — eventually became a speed-cop in America.

Everyone gave a sigh of dismay when "Sprouts" decided to return to his home country. Previously, when he agreed to ride for Southampton, he asked for, and received £1,000. After three seasons in Britain (1928-30) he had tucked away the best part of £50,000 in the bank and then, after returning to America invested it in a quick-silver mine. I believe he lost the lot.

As a Highway Patrolman at Fresno, he was critically injured in an accident and was eventually retired because of disability. Later, he was struck by a car while out walking, and was hospitalised. When his wife died, "Sprouts" took his own life.

The memory of the late Lloyd Elder is still fresh in the minds of those who saw him race ... a strange but intensely likeable character in a sport which has always been distinguished for eccentricities.

British dirt track racing in 1928 was a truly spectacular and exciting era, as also, of course, was the following season. During the first few weeks in June, 1928, there had been a remarkable increase in the interest shown by the general public. That the sport was likely to make a wide appeal was an accepted prospect. Nevertheless, even those who had followed the progress of this type of racing in Australia could not but feel surprised at the exceptionally large crowds that were now flocking to the London circuits. No less than 78,000 enthusiasts witnessed the racing at the White City on June 9, when Billy Lamont won the Silver Wings from Frank Arthur.

That initial year certainly fulfilled all that could be expected of it in the launching and establishing of dirt track racing. From its modest beginning, development had swept the country and exceeded all expectations, and by the end of 1929 there were well over seventy tracks in operation in England, Scotland and Wales. This was the original boom year.

5 The advent of league racing

The sport was still regarded as a kind of a "circus" with meetings made up of scratch and handicap races, and match races between the star riders as the special attraction. But how long would this type of meeting hold the imagination of a strong supporting public? That was the question on many promoters minds. Speedway racing had to be put on a proper, businesslike footing.

It was Jimmy Baxter — the West Ham and Southampton chief — who had the brainwave in early 1929 of forming a League, with track teams riding against each other. Although he had some opposition, he kept emphasising the fact of the urgent necessity for development on properly competitive lines. Many clear-brained promoters could see that Jimmy was right, and after much discussion a Southern League was instituted to encompass twelve fully-established tracks. These were: Stamford Bridge, Crystal Palace, West Ham, White City, Wimbledon, Harringay, Wembley, Lea Bridge, Southampton, Coventry, Perry Barr (Birmingham) and Hall Green (Birmingham). Hall Green dropped out after only a few meetings and thereafter the League remained constant with eleven teams.

Matches were originally decided over six heats, but in June this was extended to nine heats, making possible a scoring total of sixty-three points — each race then being decided on the four, two, one point system. Four riders made a team.

The Southern League Champions, captained by Gus Kuhn, won that first league championship in 1929. This photograph is a postcard readily available for sale at the time

It was not surprising in the League's early days that upsets quite frequently occurred, but none quite so effective as when in August of that season, all Overseas riders in the Star category, were barred from taking part in League events. This automatically ruled out such riders as: Vic Huxley, Billy Lamont, Frank Arthur and Max Grosskreutz.

In fairness to the Overseas contingent, English riders in the Star class were also dropped, but subsequent public appeal became so great that some of the English stars were brought back. It was, of course, a one-sided affair, and many controversies raged with the riders themselves.

However, the Stamford Bridge team, led by the redoubtable Gus Kuhn emerged from the League Championship as the winners, beating Southampton by two points. Coventry came next with the Crystal Palace fourth. Then came Wembley. Johnnie Hoskins had left the Crystal Palace, Salford and other Northern tracks and Arthur Elvin (later Sir) had appointed him as Wembley's manager. Coming late into speedway racing (May, 1929) the Wembley management had great difficulty in finding a good team to keep it going. The story of the rise of Wembley from a very shaky start to become one of the greatest of all speedway tracks, would fill a volume itself.

But speedway had its problems as early as 1929. In April a determined effort was made by local inhabitants surrounding the Harringay circuit to put an end to racing there. It was alleged that annoyance was being caused to a number of householders. International Speedways Ltd., immediately co-operated and closed all practice meetings, limiting the racing to one evening only.

Later in the season *The Star* evening paper donated two Trophies, one for the best Home rider and one for the best Overseas rider. The Championship would be run on a knock-out basis and each track management nominated a rider for competition in each section after which a series of match races would decide the two Champions. The prizes would be (in each section) the Star Trophy and £100 to the final winner and £25 to the runner-up.

The new competition got under way in late June. In September Frank Arthur defeated Vic Huxley in the final of the Overseas Section, to become the first holder of the Trophy. But it was a wonder the Home Section final ever took place. Roger Frogley had to meet Jack Parker, and Roger at that time was particularly keen on flying. Less than a week before he was due to meet Parker, he crash-landed his 'plane on the outskirts of the Flying School at Broxbourne and was very fortunate to escape with only minor injuries. However, tough-man Roger insisted in competing in the contest and defeated Jack in two straight runs. He was now the British Champion.

Jack Parker had made headline deeds throughout the season. He rode a succession of record-breaking races at tracks all over the country and his name was linked with a new record practically once every week. But there were others too who were making great names for themselves.

Colin Watson, captain of the White City (London) team, gained many honours against some of the big boys and other English riders holding their own with their Australian rivals were: Eric Spencer, Arthur Franklyn, Jim Kempster, Roger and "Buster" Frogley, Billy Dallison and "Tiger" Stevenson. Jack Barnett was the consistent star of King's Oak, and he won that track's Championship.

To my sad dismay, and certainly to the dismay of many others, the two illustrious speedway pioneers, "Buster" Frogley and Roger Frogley died in 1973 and 1974 respectively.

As far as the Overseas riders were concerned, The Big Three, "Sprouts" Elder, Frank Arthur and Vic Huxley, had maintained the positions which they established the previous year, and as far as actual successes went, there seemed to be little to choose between them. The only newcomer of any note was Max Grosskreutz who took several months to become acclimatised to the small English circuits, but he had now started to reproduce the form which had earned him the title of Australian Champion. Billy Lamont still remained the most popular rider in the country, but as was the case in 1928, he had not met with the amount of success he deserved.

One definite fact that could not be overlooked was that the 1929 season had developed very few new riders of the Championship class.

A "bad Press" in 1928 had rather given the public the impression that dirt track racing was a very low form of sport, and to dispel this unfortunate myth presented quite a problem. But fortunately, in the following year, Colonel, The Master of Sempill (later Lord Sempill) was one of those directly interested in speedway racing, and he used his influence in getting Royalty, titled people and other celebrities to attend various meetings and award the prizes.

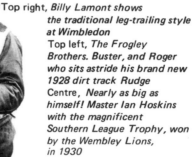

Top right, *Billy Lamont shows the traditional leg-trailing style at Wimbledon*
Top left, *The Frogley Brothers. Buster, and Roger who sits astride his brand new 1928 dirt track Rudge*
Centre, *Nearly as big as himself! Master Ian Hoskins with the magnificent Southern League Trophy, won by the Wembley Lions, in 1930*
Lower right, *Arthur Jervis, the Leicester Super Speedway captain, who in 1931 captured the European Speedway Record at 50.55mph!*
Lower left, *Winners of the 1932 National League, the Wembley Lions. From left to right; Lionel Van Praag, Reg Bounds, Ginger Lees, Colin Watson (captain), Jack Ormston, George Greenwood and Harry Whitfield*

The sport undoubtedly owes a great deal to the late Lord Sempill's early enthusiasm, and his tremendous efforts gave it a great fillip. Incidentally, in 1958, he became the original Patron of the Veteran Dirt Track Riders' Association.

Even at the beginning of the 1929 season there was no doubt that the blue and silver flat-twin Douglas was still by far the most popular and most successful dirt track machine, which for its acceleration, speed and broadsiding ability was indeed difficult to surpass. Almost without exception every rider was riding a Duggie, but there was one exception and a notable one, for the late Jim Kempster remained faithful to his illustrious Rudge Whitworth. And he won a host of trophies. The English star was affectionately known amongst his countless fans as "Smiling Jim", that quiet hero from Bedfordshire.

No machine, however good, could be expected to claim a victory in every race and, on the rare occasion, a Duggie was beaten by Frank Arthur's Harley or Kempster's Rudge.

The majority of speedway followers were not incapable of appreciating and certainly of admiring, the skill, courage and mental alertness displayed by the riders of the day. They accepted the opinions of the qualified judges such as Sir Henry Segrave, Sir Malcolm Campbell, Kaye Don, the Hon. Mrs Victor Bruce, and Sir Alan Cobham, to mention only a few who, one would have imagined, on account of their own experiences, would have been practically thrill-proof. Yet they regarded dirt track racing as a most thrilling spectacle and from time to time had expressed their sincere admiration for the riders.

Speaking generally, 1930 was a bad season all round and one of the main reasons was the abominable weather. But there were other causes; the tracks themselves; their locality or their promoters. In some cases the faults engulfed all three.

To locate the root of the trouble one had to go back to 1928, when the whole sport — with a few exceptions — was instigated it seemed from the wrong angle. Instead of building proper circuits expressly for speedway racing, some over-enthusiastic promoters seemed to imagine that they had only to spread a few loads of cinders on to the first site that was obtainable; call it a dirt track and the public would then flock through the turnstiles and make them rich people in less than no time. As grandstands were really essential, the majority of promoters followed A.J.Hunting's example and rented greyhound stadiums as their sites, which, in the main, provided "circus" turns, and not real dirt track racing, from the very start. The cinder circuits which were laid inside the greyhound tracks proved too small and the wrong shape.

During the season a number of promoters went out of business, which was no surprise; the intelligent knew it was the inevitable and welcome settling down of the sport.

The Undisputed Speedway Champion of 1930. That was the Harringay captain, Vic Huxley whose achievements reached their bizarre zenith, and, in retrospect, it is hard to imagine that supercharged ego flourishing in the climate of any other decade. He really reigned supreme and reached a pinnacle that no other rider had ever approached, winning fifteen Championships out of the seventeen contested, which included the coveted Star Championship.

Invincible Victor held fifty two track records on the thirty five tracks where he competed and was Individual Champion. He won nine £100 track Championships and later was reputed to have made £50,000 in his speedway career.

This season however, saw the start of the great England v. Australian test matches and Vic captained his Australian team in all five events, making the top score on each occasion. His earnings were around £200 to £300 per week.

Six years later, at the end of 1936, the illustrious Huxley had become tired of it all ... tired of the strain of thirteen consecutive years of racing; tired even of success. He returned to his native Australia and established a motorcycle business in Fortitude Valley, Brisbane, from which he retired eleven years ago.

Captain of the Wimbledon team for seven years; captain of the Australian test team 27 times; 34 test match appearances gaining 286 points; winner of over 140 trophies and British Individual Speedway Champion on three occasions. These were just a few of Vic Huxley's phenominal successes. When I tell you that to record even the bare bones of this man's remarkable speedway career would fill a volume, then you'll have a little idea of his fantastic racing era which lasted thirteen years.

A magnificent sportsman; an amazing rider; Vic Huxley set a standard in these qualities that was hard to surpass. Today, aged 70, he looks back over an arch of 39 years to his speedway fade-out. Even his goodbye to the game had fun and zest in it. On the final evening in February, 1937, that was to bring his racing to its virtual close; the renowned Australian pulled his last reserves of guile and effort out of the bag and scored eight points

Vic Huxley, the undisputed speedway champion of 1930

CRYSTAL PALACE SPEEDWAY TEAM 1933.
TRISS SHARP. JOE FRANCES. "NOBBY" KEY. F. E. MOCKFORD. RON JOHNSON. TOM FARNDON. HARRY SHEPHERD. GEORGE NEWTON.
MANAGING DIRECTOR. CAPTAIN.

Another postcard, the 1933 Crystal Palace team which came fourth in the National League

The late "Smiling" Jim Kempster, a famed Rudge exponent on a four-valver, and one of the greats in British speedway

(top scorer with Wally Little) in the fifth test match at Sydney.

To return to 1930. With the abolition of the "Star" status ruling, the crack riders were absorbed into the various teams, but once again, as in the previous season, the Northern League was comparatively a fiasco with many teams completing less than half their fixtures. The League consisting of Belle Vue (Manchester), the White City (Manchester), Liverpool, Preston, Warrington, Sheffield, the Leicester Super, Edinburgh, Barnsley, Newcastle, Wombwell, Rochdale and the White City (Glasgow), finished in this order.

Out of 21 matches played, Belle Vue won 19, drew one and lost one. The team was already showing signs of the supremacy that was destined to be theirs for a considerable period. Included in the side were Frank Varey, Arthur Franklyn, Eric and Oliver Langton, Dusty Haigh and Bob Harrison, while the Manchester White City team — runners-up in the League — had Frank Charles, Max Grosskreutz, Arthur Jervis, Fred Strecker and Wally Hull.

The White City circuit had been rebuilt outside the greyhound track to make it larger, and was now 446 yards round but it failed to regain its previous popularity and did not re-open the following year. In fact, it was the end of racing, for good, at this particular circuit.

The institution of the London Cup (knock-out) competition was a great success as was also the London Riders' Championship, an event still being staged today. The Wembley Lions gained the London Cup, the Southern League Championship and provided the first London Champion, Jack Ormston, who, after retiring from speedway, became a notable race horse trainer and owner in Yorkshire.

Some startling news came in mid-season for on Sunday, June 29, a number of riders fully-masked, apparently with the intention of escaping recognition, and several officials, organised a meeting at the Audenshaw trotting track in Lancashire without an ACU licence! Over twelve thousand people paid for admission and an estimated five thousand obtained free entry when the barriers were broken down! A section of the crowd was invited to go on to the centre of the circuit, and there were two narrow escapes from accidents.

The sequel however, was that the ACU, after investigating the whole matter, suspended no fewer than 34 riders and 9 officials!

The following year (1931) saw only six teams in the Northern League and, for the third time, fixtures were not completed! The finishing order was: Belle Vue, Leeds, Sheffield, Leicester Super, Preston, and Glasgow (White City). Wembley won the Southern League Championship with Stamford Bridge as runners-up.

Another trophy was put up for competition, and the first official World Championship (later re-styled the British Individual Championship) was inaugurated. Vic Huxley, still alive and well in Australia, had commenced the season as if it were a continuation of 1930. He became the World Champion, successfully defending his title against Colin Watson, a leading English rider of the day, and one who offered a strong challenge to Huxley's supremacy.

However, Vic lost his title when, at the end of the season, he was beaten by Jack Parker of the Southampton Team, but only after one of the most titanic struggles the speedway game had ever seen.

Eric Langton took the title away from Jack in 1932, after the latter had retired from the contest after breaking his collar-bone. Eric too resigned the title in the following year and Ron Johnson was awarded the title, successfully holding off a challenge by the now millionaire Claude Rye. Then "Tiger" Stevenson defeated Johnson in 1934, after which Vic Huxley defeated Stevenson. Tom Farndon then took the honour from Huxley to hold it until his tragic death at New Cross speedway in August, 1935.

Shortly after mid-season (1931), Arthur Jervis, the Leicester Super speedway captain, lowered the European record on Britain's only third of a mile track, The Super, which was managed by Alec Jackson. Arthur, clocked a time of 71.2secs., in winning the first heat of a match between Stamford Bridge and Leicester, which represented an average speed of 50.55mph! And Wal Phillips twice equalled the old European speedway record of 50.2mph. Think of it. This happened forty five years ago. Today's average on a quarter mile circuit is about the same!

As the 1932 season began, the Southern and Northern Leagues were merged into one National League. Headed by the redoubtable Colin Watson, Wembley again swept the board and Johnnie Hoskin's Lions were having their best season so far. They won the League Championship; the London Cup competition and the National Trophy. For Wembley, (originally having a very dismal start in 1929), with the institution of a Supporters' Club and an end-of-season membership of nearly 20,000, things brightened up for the Empire Stadium management, and Wembley became one of the most successful of all speedways.

1933 however, saw the start of the Belle Vue Team's domination. They had in the previous year finished third in the League, but this year the side easily won the League Championship, losing only five out of thirty six matches and they also won the National Trophy. Each season for the next three years, the National League ended with Belle Vue at the top of the chart, and it was not until 1937, when West Ham took the honours, that the unbeatable Northern side was vanquished. And this renowned team also gained the National Trophy for five successive years (1933-37).

The pioneer King's Oak track in Essex did not open for the 1933 season, much to the disappointment of its many supporters. Dwindling crowds and the increase in the rent of the track by its owners, Charringtons the brewers, were the primary causes. And the spectacular Stamford Bridge circuit at Walham Green, in SW London also closed its doors for good. Its speedway life was over ... but only after five glorious years.

This is speedway. Colin Watson, enjoying a fast ride on his Harley-JAP

6 The professional touch

One of speedway's greatest innovations came in June, 1933. Prior to this, there had been no satisfactory method of starting a race which was often chaotic. Over the years various methods were tried. Even the wily Gus Kuhn thought that perhaps he had solved the problem when he caught on a brain-wave. Like necessity, the false start was the mother of invention, and as early as April, 1932, Gus Kuhn — still a Stamford Bridge favourite — evolved a new starting device. A car pushed the four machines forward by means of a roller (bumper height) to start the engines. They were then kept on the leash (four chains) until the starting line was reached; then the car driver operated a release mechanism! But it wasn't too successful, albeit a very good idea ... by good old Gus.

The original push starts and rolling starts had caused great frustrations. The rolling-start method meant that the riders rode slowly round the track together to the starting line, the speed being regulated by the inside rider, who had not to exceed 15mph, until within four yards of the line. The starter only gave the signal for a start when all riders were in line on the four yard back line. Sometimes the riders would circle the track half a dozen times before a successful start could be made, and nothing was more annoying to the enthusiasts than these long waits, which in some instances drove the crowds away.

But the starting gate altered all that. Messrs Mockford and Smith of the Crystal Palace and Harry Shepherd, one of their contract riders, constructed a three-tape hand-operated starting gate, similar to those being used on race courses, and the necessary clutch start presented no problem, as a ruling whereby all machines had to be fitted with clutches was already in operation.

The new innovation proved an immediate success and received ACU approval. But it was not perfect. An experienced rider would watch the movement of the starter's hand and then be first into the bend. However, before the 1934 season started, this had been cured, for the Crystal Palace promoters perfected a system whereby the starting gate was electrically operated from the steward's box, out of the rider's sight. Every track was now being equipped with this type of gate, and this was the complete solution to the starting problem. After 43 years similar apparatus is, of course, still in use today.

Messrs Mockford and Smith were certainly two very enthusiastic and inventive fellows, for they later designed a track grader which automatically raised itself as it passed over the tarmac or concrete starting area.

However, with the widespread introduction of the new starting gate whereby the false start farce had been eliminated, speedway interest was on the rise again.

At the end of 1933, the wonderful Crystal Palace circuit closed down. I, like many thousands was extremely sorry to see its passing, for we had witnessed some magnificent racing on Britain's fastest quarter miler, with its sweeping, broad, banked bends. In fact it was here that I saw my first-ever speedway meeting. It was certainly a superb circuit.

The Crystal Palace contract riders; Ron Johnson, Joe Francis, Tom Farndon, George Newton, Nobby Key, and Harry Shepherd, together with a handful of Juniors, were transferred to the New Cross track, in South East London, a much smaller circuit of only 262 yards as against Crystal Palace's 440 yards, and only able to accommodate 30,000 as against the Palace's 100,000!

Instead of The Glaziers the team was now re-named The Rangers, wearing the same colours, orange and black, but with Maltese crosses on their race jackets instead of a big star. The team finished fourth in the League with Belle Vue, once again, on top.

1936 was certainly a memorable year. There was great enthusiasm in speedway racing. A Second Division

In the early thirties, Roger and Buster Frogley formed the Herts and Essex Flying Club at Broxbourne. It became the venue of many famous aviators. Here are Roger (left), Fred Mockford, Amy Johnson, Jim Mollison, Buster's wife Hetty and Buster himself

Two famous promoters — a classic shot, Johnnie Hoskins in suit and Jack Hill-Bailey in Fair Isle at a 1930 King's Oak meeting

was instituted. The First Division comprised Belle Vue, Wembley, Harringay, Hackney Wick, Wimbledon, New Cross and West Ham (who finished the season in that order) and the Second Division included Southampton, Bristol, Nottingham, Liverpool and Plymouth. This two-League system operated right up to and including 1939. But initially Division Two seemed doomed to failure — at least until a diminutive Californian arrived in England. It was Putt Mossman who came over from New Zealand with his team of American speedway riders, and they were motorcycle stunt-men too, of high repute. Putt's individual acts were not dissimilar to those of today's Evel Knievel, and this ace stunt rider appeared at Hackney Stadium. He raced his motorcycle down a prepared, inclined plank, from the top of the stand into a tank of fire with less than fifteen inches of water in it. Putt escaped with a broken nose and pluckily rode around the track to reassure spectators it was nothing worse!

    Breath-taking acts were, of course, his speciality: he would climb up and down a ladder fixed to the rear of his machine travelling at 30mph, finding the even torque of his 4-cylinder Harley-Davidson an immense stabilising help when performing this particular stunt — just another of his playful habits.

Putt Mossman's circus consisted of his wife Helen, Dessie Grant, Byrd McKinney who later rode for Wimbledon; Ray Grant (the 1933 USA Champion), Manuel Trujillo, a real Mexican who was as good at playing a guitar as riding a motorcycle; Sam Arena, Bo Lisman, Ewald Schnitzer, Pete Coleman and Pee Wee Cullum, the midget of the team, who rode for Belle Vue in two post-war seasons.

The Troupe, the most extraordinary the sport has ever known, was busily engaged in staging shows at most National, Provincial and Amateur speedways, to the tune of sixty performances. Not only did it help to fill in blank evenings at several tracks, but sometimes their regular attendances were doubled. Above all, Putt and his merry men saved many a Second Division track from extinction. Yes, speedway racing certainly owed a lot to Putt Mossman and his Crazy Gang.

Another notable highlight of 1936 was the arrival for the first time of the Milne brothers, Jack and Cordy, from the States, who were both signed by New Cross. The fans had not seen any Americans for many years, not since the fabulous "Sprouts" Elder, Art Pechar and Ray Tauser. But the ACU said "No. Two riders of this calibre will make New Cross much too strong." And so Cordy went to Hackney Wick.

The Milnes were magnificent in the extreme. Speedway attendances immediately increased; some of our established stars were beaten by the American pair ... and all was well with British speedway racing.

There were now many international riders in the country and the first World Championship with FIM approval was instituted. It was won by the Australian ace, Lionel Van Praag of the Wembley team, after an exhilarating deciding tussle with Eric Langton. "Bluey" Wilkinson was third.

Wimbledon had three of the American riders in the country for 1937. Wilbur Lamoreaux (who died in 1963 at the comparatively young age of 55), Benny Kaufman and Miny Waln. Benny was a little fellow who always looked spruce and clean but he failed to reach the topmost heights. Miny was perhaps an even greater disappointment; a great trier, he could not settle down on the English circuits and disappeared as the season ended. Later, he became a boss at the American Lockheed Aircraft Company and invested some of his capital in 90 acres of apricots at Hemet, California. A boom came round; he sold out and made a fortune!

"Lammy" Lamoreaux, one of the quiet boys of speedway, starting riding at the Los Angeles track in 1932. Coming to England in '37 with a notable reputation he became one of the greatest riders in the sport, finishing runner-up to Jack Milne in the 1937 World Championship Final. He was third in the following year's event. Wilbur was a skilful and courageous rider and certainly a daring little guy. When he returned to the States he became a successful motorcycle dealer in Glendale.

Speeds were becoming faster; the game more tougher. Even so the 1938 season proved a magnificent one. Four or five years previous the critics were predicting the early demise of speedway racing, but they were wrong, and this season in particular was one of the most successful in the eleven years' British history of the sport. Official attendances up to the end of August at First and Second Division tracks totalled the astonishing figure of 2,590,011. First Division tracks averaged around fifteen thousand per meeting, which was a remarkable figure.

There was greater and much keener competition. At one time the Wembley "Lions" were practically unbeatable. Then the Belle Vue Aces made an even cleaner sweep of top honours from 1933 to 1937. Now the position was different and, for the first time, the New Cross team became National League Champions. They were worthy of the honour and the work of the mechanics, Tommy Hall and Alf Cole had as much as anything to do with the winning of the Championship.

Their first-class behind the scenes organisation and their gallant fight after a heavy casualty list deserved the highest praise. The New Cross side had included Stan Greatrex (Captain), Jack Milne, Clem Mitchell, Bill Longley, Ernie Evans, Ron Johnson, George Newton and Joe Francis. The latter two were seriously injured, while at one time or another, three of the others had been ill. However, in spite of all these setbacks, overall, New Cross were the best combination of men and machines, although towards the end of the season, Wimbledon shot to the fore, winning the much-coveted London Cup, the National Trophy, and the South London Championship.

The story of how "Bluey" Wilkinson, a far from fit man, realised his ambition and won the World Championship is certainly a highlight of history. The previous evening, when competing in the final of a New Cross scratch race, his front wheel appeared to twist underneath his machine and the West Ham rider was thrown over the handlebars and suffered a nasty shoulder injury. However, the next evening a record crowd of 90,000 turned up at Wembley to see the gallant ginger-headed boy from Bathurst (New South Wales), when in great pain, defeat the American aces, Jack Milne and Wilbur Lamoreaux into second and third places respectively and be crowned World Champion of 1938.

NEW CROSS TEAM 1934.

HARRY SHEPHERD. ROY DOOK. STAN GREATREX. GEORGE NEWTON.
JOE FRANCIS. TOM FARNDON. F. E. MOCKFORD. RON JOHNSON. NOBBY KEY.

The 1934 New Cross team which came third in the National League of that year.

Putt Mossman, the famous American, who with his team of riders, all stuntmen too, saved many a Second Division track from extinction in 1936. Here he is on his in-line 4 cylinder Harley-Davidson

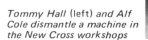

Tommy Hall (left) and Alf Cole dismantle a machine in the New Cross workshops

Two riders, two styles. Dick Reynolds leads Bob Jones, in an exciting race at Oxford Speedway in 1938. Both rode dirt track Rudges

Unfortunately the courageous "Bluey" Wilkinson was not seen racing in England in 1939, apart from a special charity appearance, for he took on the role of promoter at Sheffield. In that single come-back appearance, in a match with Arthur Atkinson, "Bluey" won in two straight runs and broke West Ham's track record in the process. From the hands of the Duchess of Kent he received his last Trophy.

At the end of '39 "Bluey" returned to his native land and joined the Australian Forces as World War Two had started. He spent his last evening in this country with Johnnie Hoskins — the West Ham chief — who gave a farewell party. On July 27, 1940, "Bluey", once the idol of a million fans, was motorcycling home from the pictures with his wife on the pillion, when on the outskirts of Sydney he collided with a motor truck, the driver of which had swerved to avoid a car which had suddenly pulled out of a side road. It was not "Bluey's" fault, but tragically, the accident had cost him his life, and one of the greatest figures in speedway racing had been lost for good.

1939 however, saw many changes. Southampton came into Division One, and Bristol returned to Division Two. Birmingham, Leeds, Lea Bridge and the West Ham "Hawks" dropped out of the Second Division with the Belle Vue reserves stepping in. The seven-team National League, the same number which had been in existence since '35, could not complete its fixtures but here are the teams in order of finishing as at September 1. Belle Vue, Wimbledon, Wembley, West Ham, Harringay, Southampton and New Cross. Newcastle won the Division Two contest which Hackney Wick had previously won the year before. Bristol had taken the honours in '37 and Southampton in '36.

After twelve years of trial and endeavour the sport, in 1939, stood on the threshold of a great future. It had definitely come to stay, but World War Two had unfortunately broken out and that was that ... for the time being.

Speedway stadiums reluctantly put up their shutters. Riders exchanged their colourful race-jackets for khaki, navy and air-force blue, and, with supporters and all the rest, went forth to battle with the enemy.

Six long years had to elapse before National speedway racing was resumed.

7 The war-time years

For a management to stage speedway meetings while World War Two was being fought, presented almost unsurmountable difficulties but, when every other speedway in the country closed down for the war years (September 1939-1945) apart from an isolated meeting at West Ham and Southampton at Easter 1940, Belle Vue miraculously remained open throughout. The World Championship Final, just on the point of being decided; the National Trophy Final between Belle Vue and Wembley, and many other fixtures were unavoidably and immediately cancelled.

Speedway racing attracted and, of course, still attracts, the best type of sportsman and sportswomen. There was very serious work for everyone just now; the sport could be enjoyed as and when the opportunity occurred again, but the country's need came first and foremost.

Promoters and riders were certainly doing their bit, and doing it well. Two prominent managerial figures, Cecil Smith of New Cross speedway and Richard Maybrook of Wimbledon were recruiting the Despatch Riding Section of the London Fire Brigade and from the Wimbledon enthusiasts, over seven hundred enlisted.

Many riders and officials joined up too, but most went into the Forces. Others found employment for their mechanical skill in the aircraft and munition workshops. George Greenwood, once a team member of the Wembley Lions, joined the RAF. Today, of course, he is head of the JAP engine concern. George Pepper, (Newcastle's pre-war brilliant Canadian skipper) became one of Britain's best night fighter pilots, and won the DFC, before losing his life in a non-operational crash.

Morian Hansen, speedway's 'Great Dane', who became a squadron leader, gained the George Medal as well as the DFC. The British George Medal was also awarded to former World Champion (1936) Lionel Van Praag, a member of the Royal Australian Air Force, for great gallantry in helping his co-pilot save the lives of two fellow members of the crew, one a non-swimmer and the other semi-conscious, after their aircraft had been shot down and sunk in the Timor Sea. This was in 1942, and between them, supporting and towing the injured man and the non-swimmer, the party reached shore after being in the icy water for thirty hours, during which time they had beaten off several attacks by sharks.

George Newton's mechanic, the late Alfred Cole, became a Divisional Fire Officer in charge of dispatch riders in the London Region, while Ronnie Greene, the Wimbledon Manager, held the post of Assistant Fire Force Commander and he later received the MBE for his valuable services. Fred Mockford, of New Cross speedway, was awarded the George Medal for his deeds during the 1940-41 German "Blitz."

The Belle Vue management however, continued meetings well into October, 1939. Then came a short break owing to the government's ruling regarding the gathering of crowds; nevertheless, 597 meetings had been organised at the famous track since its opening on March 23, 1929. Incidentally, Belle Vue's track in 1928, was a different one, a little further along Hyde Road, at the greyhound stadium.

As soon as the crowd ban rule was relaxed, Belle Vue continued to organise its race meetings. The speedway flag was certainly being kept flying in Manchester and the track became the meeting place for large numbers of persons who had an interest in speedway racing. Every Saturday during the summer, riders from all over the country would head for Manchester, and although their numbers grew progressively less, as the effects of war

Morian Hansen, speedway's "Great Dane" was a Squadron Leader in World War Two and gained the British George Medal as well as the DFC

grew greater, the BV management, somehow or other, amazingly still carried on. And when the total number of enthusiasts were totted up as the war ended, it was found that no less than 2,816,000 people had attended 170 war-time meetings, staged between 1940 and 1945 inclusively!

The riders included the ever-faithful Belle Vue group — Frank Varey, Bill Kitchen, Oliver Hart and Eric and Oliver Langton, Jack and Norman Parker, Bill Pitcher, Les Wotton, Ron Johnson, Tommy Price, Eric Chitty and Ron Clarke, all made regular appearances. Some of the stars who were in the Forces, like Morian Hansen, Malcolm Craven, Ernie Price, Jack Gordon, Eric Gregory, Ron Mason, Bill Kitchen and Geoff Godwin, etc., raced as often as they were able.

The extremely difficult organisation of these meetings was in the very capable hands of Alice Hart, the country's first-ever speedway lady manageress/promoter and her reward was a place on Belle Vue's board of Directors.

It was typical of her that she insisted that only the best was good enough for Belle Vue speedway, and making sure of it by personal supervision. Later Miss Hart took up track interests in Sheffield and Edinburgh with Frank Varey.

Included in Alice Hart's activities at the Manchester track was the compiling of the Belle Vue speedway bulletins which besides Britain, were sent to enthusiasts all over the world, and these bulletins included the previous meeting's results. This was, incidentally, the sport's only war-time magazine.

Alice Hart had the thankless task of waiting to see just who were the riders who were going to turn up each Saturday. Had any of them had their leave cancelled? Had any of the trains in which they were travelling been held up through enemy action? These were just two of Miss Hart's worries. On top of this she had the organisation part to do.

The riders had many difficulties too. Everyone of them, most dedicated to the sport, were prepared to suffer a host of inconveniences. Remember there was no petrol for pleasure purposes, and cars were prohibited to be used for transporting machines. But difficulties are made to overcome, and they certainly were, albeit in various inventive ways.

The only way for most of the boys to have Saturdays off was to work until late in the evening or work all day on Sundays — perhaps for nothing! Having obtained the necessary time off, and a ticket to Manchester, it was really no guarantee that they would arrive there! They may have had to stand all the way, with carriages being full to the brim or even sit on the floor in the guard's van. This was perhaps unique in speedway history, for the railways really held a monopoly!

Speedway machines cluttering up the guard's van, with a war being fought. Surely the two didn't go together? Many railway officials took a very dim view of this particular situation and were not backward in their abuses towards the riders. To travel by rail was certainly an extremely hectic and very unpleasant business. Even the porters remained indifferent; they were reluctant to allow any machines in the guard's van ... and so the story went on.

On one occasion however, Ron Clarke had a big row to get his bikes on the train and, after being successful in the end, found that his machines had ended up on the platform again when he looked out of the window shortly after the train had started! But jovial Eric Chitty had an answer to that the following week, when he produced a six foot length of chain. After a few minutes skirmish with a porter, which was eventually won, out came the chain. Eric chained the bikes to the side of the guard's van and Fred Tuck remarked: "They'll have to unhook the truck now!"

Transport was one problem for the rider. There was another regarding spare parts for the machines, because after the war had been going on for a year, engine spares were practically non-existent. The prices of those that were available rocketed sky-high. Unfortunately for the boys it was "pay up" or no racing. Difficult days ... hard days ... frustrating days, indeed. But for Belle Vue, speedway racing had to go on!

The Belle Vue circuit itself certainly had some rough treatment during those six long years, and the way it stood up to things was quite amazing. As I have said there was no pleasure petrol ... no petrol even for the grader, which was having a well-earned rest in its garage. Even so, with additional work being put on the rakers, the track was never what one could call very rough. Someone humourously suggested borrowing an elephant from the adjoining Zoo, to pull the grader on one occasion when the circuit became a little rough. A good idea, but I have no knowledge that it ever came off!

Tommy Price, Eric Chitty and Fred Tuck were always out to enjoy themselves, as were other riders too. They would sit in the guard's van with their machines, each one waiting for the other to open his sandwich bag first. Tommy always had the best selection, so the other two always waited for him! Arriving at Manchester station, a taxi took them to the stadium. After the meeting a taxi made the return journey, and as many as eleven riders often used to pile into one taxi, giving the driver just ten minutes to reach the station!

Riders like the Canadian, Eric Chitty, Bill Kitchen, Norman Parker and Eric Langton met with great racing successes at Belle Vue and many others improved their pre-war form.

The majority of the meetings consisted of Individual Championships with Best Pairs contests and other Trophy events thrown in. There were also a few team matches during 1943, and in 1944 a miniature league was

Eric Chitty, the Canadian, at one time West Ham skipper, made several appearances at Belle Vue during war-time and won several "championship" events

formed in which the Belle Vue team, assisted by several guest riders, met the Opposition side. The home team claimed nineteen matches.

The premier event each season however, was the British Individual Championship, staged on modified World Championship lines. Eric Chitty, one of the great favourites at Belle Vue, gained the Title three times in succession, 1940-1942, besides other successes such as the Northern Championship in 1942 and the All-England Best Pairs contest with Fred Tuck as his partner, in the following year. The British Individual Championship was taken away from Eric in 1943 by Ron Clarke — he failed to qualify for the Final. Ron later became an Odsal star.

Miss Hart, chief of the Belle Vue management, and her assistants, had to be heartily congratulated in having successfully overcome some formidable obstacles in keeping the sport alive. The programme issued reassured everyone that no petrol whatsoever was used. The fuel was, in fact, wood alcohol and the contents of every competitor's tank was tested!

The speedway Derby held during the Whitsun holiday in 1944 is well worth relating. It proved that the sport had certainly not lost any of its public appeal, in spite of the fact that spectacular performances were not quite so high as they were before the war, due to circumstances beyond the riders' control. Nevertheless, as this was a stay-at-home holiday, the support was almost entirely composed of local enthusiasts, and although bigger crowds had been seen, this event attracted a crowd of twelve thousand on the Monday. How everyone arrived there remained much of a mystery!

The machines on view were, of course, 1939 speedway models or before, but there was a 1932 Excelsior-JAP which created plenty of interest. There had been a great amount of scheming and contriving to make the machines fit for track racing, and many riders all said the same thing (as spares were unobtainable) that makeshift substitutes had to be devised. It was evident that some very ingenious work had been done in making frames serviceable, despite high-tensile steel tubing being unprocurable. Tyres were being made to last many times beyond their normal life, and ignition troubles were aggravated by the use of inferior substitute fuel.

These things, with others, of course, made one realise that this was a war-time effort, and a very big one too, staged under the greatest of difficulties, and only made possible by that unquenchable enthusiasm for the motorcycle sport.

Actually there were two Whitsun meetings. On Saturday and on Monday. In the Saturday one, Norman Parker, attempted to break the 4-lap clutch start record, held jointly by Van Praag and Eric Langton at 74secs. And he was successful. He clocked 73.25secs.

It was Norman Parker too who took the honours in Monday's speedway Derby. He had shared the distinction

Bill Kitchen — the overnight sensation of 1933 — starred at the Manchester circuit winning the Belle Vue Grand Prix in 1941

with Eric Chitty of being the leader two days previous in the main event — the Grand Prix. Firstly, there was a match race in which Oliver Hart and Les Wotton took part, but Oliver's engine trouble spoilt his effort. Les's return to speedway was welcome. He had recently been discharged from the RAF, but unfortunately was off form in the Derby, in which sixteen riders took part. The Final result was: Norman Parker 12 points, Jack Parker 11, Tommy Price 10, Frank Varey 10, Eric Gregory 9, Wally Lloyd 7, Ron Clarke 6, Ron Johnson 6, Wilf Plant 5, Tommy Allott 5, Norman Evans 2 and Les Wotton 2. Fastest time of day: Tommy Price, 76secs. Records were, however, out of the question, since it soon became obvious that shortcomings in maintenance of machines, quite unavoidable for a number of reasons, imposed limitations which no amount of riding skill could overcome.

Thus ended a most successful two-day affair, actually the 121 st., war-time meeting. There were 49 more still to come! And then Belle Vue justifiably boasted ... "We never closed," the only speedway to claim that distinction.

Everyone associated with the sport owed a great debt to Miss Hart and her batch of staunch assistants for keeping speedway racing alive through those dark and dismal years. But apart from the war period, Belle Vue has always been a hot-bed of racing. In fact, more meetings have been staged at Hyde Road, Manchester than at any other track in the world. A continuous run from Belle Vue's first meeting at the greyhound stadium on July 28, 1928, to the present day is certainly a superb longevity record.

One day, in March, 1946, when Arthur Atkinson (West Ham's joint promoter with Stanley Greatrex) was digging up the West Ham track, he unearthed a small object which, on being cleaned, proved to be a German Iron Cross. That stadium was, of course, used as a transit camp for the troops embarking for D Day operations in 1944, but it had never accommodated prisoners of war or homeward bound troops. The only feasible explanation of this remarkable find was that the Iron Cross must have fallen from the air when a German 'plane was shot down in the vicinity of the stadium.

THE WAR-TIME CHAMPIONS AT BELLE VUE
1940 to 1945

BRITISH INDIVIDUAL CHAMPIONSHIP

	Winner	*Second place*
1940	Eric Chitty	Bill Pitcher
1941	Eric Chitty	Bill Kitchen
1942	Eric Chitty	Frank Varey
1943	Ron Clarke	Bill Kitchen
1944	Frank Varey	Jack Parker
1945	Bill Kitchen	Tommy Price & Eric Chitty

NORTHERN CHAMPIONSHIP		**TRACK CHAMPIONSHIP**	**INTERNATIONAL TROPHY**
1940	Bill Kitchen	—	—
1941	Oliver Hart		
1942	Eric Chitty	Oliver Hart	Bill Longley
1943	Norman Parker	Frank Varey	—
1944	Norman Parker	Eric Gregory	Norman Parker
1945	Alec Statham	Norman Parker	Bill Longley

BELLE VUE GRAND PRIX		**BELLE VUE SPEEDWAY DERBY**
1940	Eric Langton & Frank Varey	Jack Parker
1941	Bill Kitchen	Frank Varey
1942	Eric Chitty	Bill Longley
1943	Norman Parker	—
1944	Norman Parker	Norman Parker
1945	Tommy Price	Jack Parker & Tommy Price (Best Pairs)

BRITISH EMPIRE BEST PAIRS		**ALL ENGLAND BEST PAIRS**
1940	—	Eric Langton & Frank Varey
1941	Eric Langton & Frank Varey	Ron Johnson & Eric Chitty
	Bill Kitchen & Oliver Hart	
1942	Frank Varey & Bill Kitchen	Bill Kitchen & Oliver Hart
1943	Bill Kitchen & Oliver Hart	Eric Chitty & Fred Tuck
1944	Eric Chitty & Ron Clarke	—
1945	Jack Parker & Bill Pitcher	Ron Johnson & Alec Statham

THE NATIONAL TROPHY		**THE SPEEDWAY CUP**
1941	Bill Kitchen & Oliver Hart	Bill Kitchen & Oliver Hart
1942	Ron Johnson	Eric Langton & Frank Varey
1943	Norman Parker & Les Wotton	Frank Varey
1944	Eric Chitty	Oliver Hart & Les Wotton

THE HUNDRED GUINEAS TROPHY

1942	Eric Chitty	1945	Ron Johnson

8 The post-war years

Although 1946 marked the resumption of National League racing for the first time since 1939, New Cross had staged a few meetings in '45, the initial one being on June 27. And on this occasion an estimated 10,000 enthusiasts were turned away when the stadium became full. It was just a prelude to what would be happening the following season, when full-scale racing would begin.

With hostilities over, the sport came back with a bang. Entertainment-starved, with the fears and worries of war now firmly in the background, fans flocked in an unprecedented scale to see speedway racing once again. The stadium turnstiles worked overtime and through them streamed thousands and thousands of enthusiasts, after waiting patiently for over six years to see the return of their own spectacular blood-stirring sport, a sport so free of stigma of any kind, that attracts the right kind of public.

The great pulse of the crowds beat faster in every stadium throughout the country as they heard the wild music of impatient motors, whose song had been stifled for so long. Racing was certainly back with a vengeance! The old familiar coloured berets, badges, scarves and rattles reappeared and, once again, programmes were waved in the air.

Records show that from April until the end of September (1946) more than 6,500,000 fans attended meetings of the dozen operational tracks! 2,500,000 more than in 1938 — the previous best. 57,000 at West Ham's opening meeting — a friendly match against Wembley who won by a single point; 50,000 at Wembley and 25,000 at New Cross and Belle Vue. Bomb-scarred Wimbledon opened on Good Friday and thousands had to be turned away. When its last meeting of the season took place, the gates were finally closed with 30,000 inside and police remonstrated with hundreds that were, once again, locked out! Moreover, it was just a friendly match — the Dons v. the Wembley Lions!

Capacity crowds were commonplace all over the country ... it was enthusiasm really boiling over!

Riders had been 'pooled' to ensure equable distribution of talent, but an introduced grading system was abolished after six weeks, when riders clearly showed their disapproval.

There were, however, two Leagues, the Southern and the Northern, the former consisting of Wembley, Belle Vue, Bradford, Wimbledon, New Cross and West Ham, and the latter of Middlesbrough, Sheffield, Norwich, Birmingham, Newcastle and Glasgow. And they finished the League tables in that order.

Of course, it was a superb season of sport. Every attendance record had been smashed, and the same thing happened in grass track racing.

The idea of speedway being staged at Bradford's Odsal stadium amazed many, for several promoters decided that the project was impossible. But then, Johnnie Hoskins had been amazing us for years and he opened the new track in mid-season 1945 with Colin Watson making the fastest time. The circuit of 410 yards was the most banked in the country — four feet on the bends, and, like Belle Vue, there was no intervening greyhound course.

To Johnnie's keen business eye, its possibilities were obvious. Situated in a heavily populated industrial area and with stadium accommodation capable of holding crowds up to 100,000 he quickly seized the chance. And speedway at Odsal was an immediate success, due largely to his showmanship.

From a modest beginning he built up local support until Saturday evening meetings were drawing up to 40,000. By '46 Odsal had a team which was skippered by Alex Statham and the brilliance of its senior riders was highlighted by the fact that they were better represented in the Riders' Championship Final than any other side.

Replacing the World Championship Final, the British Riders' Championship was instituted and 85,000 fans

Reg Lambourne, Swindon Speedway's first captain (left) chats with teamster, vice-captain Bob Jones and managing director Reg Witcomb, following final trials

The 1950 Walthamstow team. Left to right, Harry Edwards, Ron Lewin (trainer), Bert Edwards, Reg Reeves, Arch Windmill, Benny King, George Newton, John Deeley (manager), Charlie May and Jim Boyd - captain (on machine)

The Australian, Ron Johnson, idol of the New Cross fans 'down the Old Kent Road'

flocked to the Empire Stadium Wembley. As was so often the case in big competitions, the meeting sprang a surprise on everyone. The favourites, Jack Parker, Eric Langton and Ron Johnson, all fell by the wayside while, steady, determined Tommy Price went on to a well-deserved victory.

Speedway racing had always had an extremely hard battle to gain proper recognition by the Press. The fact that nearly a half million applications were received for the 85,000 available seats at Wembley, made even the most somnolent Editors in Fleet Street stir in their sleep and divert their attention from endless columns of football, golf and horse racing, to the more spectacular sport on the cinders.

Dick Southhouse, then the manager of the Control Board, received dozens of applications for new tracks to be constructed, a season reminiscent of early 1929. Cardiff, Leeds, Liverpool, Coventry, Sunderland, Edinburgh, Portsmouth and Southampton were just waiting for the go-ahead, as and when the shortage of materials situation improved.

It was in 1945 too that the new Speedway Riders' Association was inaugurated with Ivor Pole as Secretary, and the evergreen Jack Parker as Chairman. For the first time the SRA received a membership of practically 100%.

When you realise that in 1946 nearly 1,250,000 enthusiasts packed the stands and terraces at Wembley alone, you could see that speedway racing, once dubbed the Cinderella of motorcycle sport, had truly grown up.

1946 was certainly a boom year. But '47 proved even greater. For the first time in history the National League (to allow for fifteen new tracks) was extended to three Divisions. The old National League became Division One; the Northern League, which now included Bristol and Wigan, was named the Second Division, while the new track promotions became Division Three.

The re-opening of the Harringay track strengthened the First Division and the North London management were more than delighted to have secured the services (by direct negotiation) of three Australians, Vic Duggan, his brother Ray and Frank Dolan. All three, plus Cliff Parkinson, arrived in mid-April at London Airport together with their machines, and these were the first-ever riders to fly from Australia.

Vic Duggan was, of course, no newcomer to this country, for he had been a pre-war team member of Hackney Wick, Wimbledon and Bristol, but had yet to reach the highest of heights. However, he was the Australian Champion in '45 and he was destined to gain the Title again in '47 and '48. But on his first English appearances it was obvious that Vic was out to stir up the game; no one could have forecast such phenomenal performances from one man. Maximum scores flew off his rear wheel as readily as the cinders; a super ace had certainly arrived. It was to be Vic Duggan's year.

Not since the mighty Vic Huxley had we seen such an artist in skill and speed. The cool confidence and daring polished tactics of this great Australian with the crisp, wavy hair, liberally streaked with grey, became a saga of the speedways as Vic regularly met, and defeated, the aces of the day. To defeat him meant headlines for the winner, but elite indeed were the few who could repeat the performance.

Riding a machine which he built and practically maintained himself, the fabulous "Black Duck" gained nearly every honour that speedway had to offer. Tremendous crowds flocked to see him ride — the spectacular and phenomenally successful Australian was something new in speedway. Vic rode undefeated for Harringay through 16 out of 24 League matches; he won the London Riders' Championship; he was Australia's top-scorer in all three Tests; he gained the Match Race Title and the Wimbledon Laurels. These were but a few of his successes, and when the season was over, Australia's Miracle Man had won 297 firsts; 39 seconds; three thirds and one fourth out of 348 starts! He had gained 972 points out of a possible 1044! The dynamic Victor John Duggan had put new life into British speedway.

1947 proved to be, in the complete history of the sport, its greatest year. For two more seasons it would still be enjoying its boom period. For the immense crowds it was a diversion from the monotonous routine of everyday life. But hard times lay ahead for the sport, from which only its strongest adherents were to survive.

Unaware of the troubles to come ... 1949 raced on unabatedly. But unfortunately the bubble was showing a sign of bursting, just a tiny one, for Hull in the Third Division gave up the ghost in mid-season, and the Swindon management who was plodding along with team building in its first-ever season, immediately took over the East Yorkshire fixtures and its riders, which included Mick Mitchell, Alf Webster, Derek Glover and George Craig.

Not in the entire history of speedway racing had any one rider held an Individual Title of the Match Race Championship size for so long and against so many challengers as the ever-green Jack Parker. In defeating Ron Johnson in two straight runs at New Cross and similarly at Belle Vue, Jack eliminated his thirteenth challenger in the two years and ten months he had held the Golden Helmet Title. In that time he had been beaten just once!

The late Ray and Vic Duggan (standing), the illustrious brothers from Australia. 1947 was Vic's year — not since Vic Huxley had there been seen such an artist

The "Laughing Boy" of speedway, Oliver Hart was the greatest and the last of the leg-trailers, post-war; his immensely spectacular broadsiding was always a crowd pleaser

The dynamic Graham Warren from Australia was a Birmingham teamster

An established Wembley favourite was "Split" Waterman who made his initial cinder debut in Italy

Jack, then the 43 year old veteran skipper of the Belle Vue Aces and England, was also the undisputed paternal head of the sport, and he headed the points list with a total of 367 scored in 38 matches!

Speedway racing is, and always has been, a serious business, but it is not without its lighter moments. Take, for instance, Swindon's first-ever meeting in 1949 at Blunsdon. A Doctor, a complete newcomer to speedway, was in attendance, and before the match he was, incongruously, directed to the pits to examine all the riders to see that they were fit to race. Espying a group of fellows wearing white jerseys, he lined them up and in accordance with the request, raised their jerseys for heart-testing and said nothing. But the third man, not unnaturally, enquired: "What is all this for?" The conscientious Doctor, in serious vein, replied that he was only carrying out instructions. "But we're not Riders, we're Rakers!" came the exclamation to a confused and rather astonished Doctor. Hardly believable, but nevertheless, true.

How many enthusiasts know that speedway racing has its own Motto — and almost since its inception? Not many I guess! But it has — and the sport in 1929 was indebted to the Hon. Mrs Forbes Sempill — later Lady Sempill — not only for the original suggestion that the game was worthy of an appropriate Motto, but for the Latin Motto itself. Fortitudine ac Virtute, which, translated into English, means By Endurance and Valour.

Even the most casual observer appreciates the fact that speedway racing demands amongst other admirable qualities, high courage and powers of endurance far above the ordinary, and it is the possession of these qualities which enables any rider who has the natural riding ability to reach the top of the tree.

The yearly total attendances are interesting: 1946, (13 tracks), 6,623,587. 1947, (23 tracks) 9,238,660. 1948 (29 tracks) 10,694,361 and 1949, (34 tracks) 12,500,000. In this latter year over £500,000 was paid in entertainment tax (later abolished) by speedway promoters.

By 1950 the number of British tracks in the three Divisions amounted to 37 and the same number existed in the following year, but only 35 survived and the sport started to head towards its lowest ebb. The boom was over.

Combining the fact that there was generally a shortage of money and with the cost of living skyrocketing, attendances came down with a bump. And actually the same happened in grass track racing, its biggest-ever boom and then the inevitable slump. It had to happen. Nothing could stop it. New Cross closed its doors in June, 1953, because of lack of support. The Rangers chief, Fred Mockford, who had been promoting the cinder sport for 26 years said: "I cannot keep on losing money." He gave the reasons as; the increasing popularity of television; the high entertainment tax; higher rents, rates, transport charges; the lack of thrills in speedway; restriction on foreign riders and the lack of new riders, especially in the First Division. "Each one of these represents, a nail in the New

The greatest speedway brotherhood. Jack and Norman Parker, the former one time skipper of Belle Vue, the latter of Wimbledon

A 1972 picture of Barry Briggs with his enormous collection of trophies. The large one in the centre is the Sunday Dispatch World Speedway Championship Trophy

The three greatest New Zealand riders, Ronnie Moore (left), Ivan Mauger (centre) and Barry Briggs in 1973

Cross coffin. I think we should go back to dirt track racing, with not less than six inches of top cinder dressing. The biggest mistake made, was to go in for hard shale tracks."

The previous items listed by Fred Mockford, that caused the New Cross downfall, could likewise be attributed to many other promotions who were forced to close.

It was however, a fact that at New Cross, many supporters drifted away when their idol, Ron Johnson began to fade. This certainly was a contributory factor for Ron was such a prime favourite, a magnificent rider too, and how the fans loved him! He had, of course, been with Fred since joining the Crystal Palace, early in 1928.

Over the years, many different views and schemes had been put forward in an endeavour to provide exciting and closer racing. Ken Brett, team manager of West Ham and one of its former riders, had an idea which was quite simple. He would like to see all tracks equipped with two starting gates. "Races are won and lost at the starting gate ... first out, first home in eight cases out of ten" he said. "That's the trouble."

Ken's plan was to erect a second gate, roughly a bike's length behind the first, and they would be synchronised. Head leaders would start from slots 1 and 2 at the rear gate while second strings would get away from the front gate in slots 3 and 4. The arrangement could be changed so that the "big boys" occupied slots 3 and 4 (at the rear gate) in alternative races.

Thus, claimed Ken, the spectacle of speedway would be improved and I agreed with him. He remarked; "This could be the medicine to cure the sport's main bugbear, dull, flat, lifeless and processional racing." It was put to Ken that some of the stars might object to such a form of handicapping, but outspoken Brett replied; "Far too many of them are taking too much out of the game ... those who object to starting a machine's length behind should be told to get out."

But, much to Ken Brett's disappointment, no one took the trouble to carry the proposition out, and in the end a superb brain wave was just forgotten.

"Split" Waterman of Harringay was perhaps the most popular rider of '53. He was out to give the crowd a show in every race. That made him the ideal speedway rider. He got quite a kick out of racing, and the financial side, useful though it was, didn't rule his enthusiasm.

A fine ambassador for the sport, "Split" embodied the very essence of speedway — he had personality, skill, and dare-devilry of the highest order, which tended to make him the sport's number-one showman. As the English Captain for every England v Australia Test Match that season and runner-up in the World Championship, "Split" was one of the most colourful personalities.

He had, of course, made his debut for Wembley in '47 and was an immediate success. Transferred in the 1949-50 close season on his own request to Harringay for £3,000, proved a transfer fee record as riders had never changed hands for over £2,000. Born in New Malden, Surrey, and christened Squire, he acquired the nickname of "Split" while previously racing on Army tracks in Italy. On his return to England he had a meteoric rise to fame.

One of his greatest individual victories was achieved at New Cross in '48 when he defeated 15 of the best riders in the London area, to carry off the coveted London Rider's Championship. The 31 year old rider, in '51, took the Golden Helmet Match Race Champion title away from Jack Parker, who had held it for two years — a record in itself. Dynamic "Split" then defended it against two of the top riders of the day, Aub Lawson and Jack Young.

1954, and the crowds were still drifting away from speedway. The League Teams were down to only 19. In five more years they would be down to 9. The fact that speedway racing was dying could not be overlooked, in fact it stared everyone in the face. So what could be done? No one seemed to have very much initiative ... and Ken Brett's brain-child was not even tried out. Had we seen too much of the highly-skilled short-wheelbased riding and not enough spectacular broadsiding? That was one of the big questions.

Lionel Wills, one of the pioneers of the sport in 1928 at the Crystal Palace made this remark: "The sport has lost its kick. We have got to get the spectacle back again into speedway. Let the riders return to the leg-trailing technique, with handlebars bent downwards in true racing style. The search for speed has, in fact only increased speeds about 7% in the last 20 years. An average race at West Ham is now won at 45mph, against 42mph, in 1930.

Tommy Price, Eric Williams, Eric Langton, to name but a few, advocated a return to leg-trailing but, surprisingly, "Tiger" Stevenson and Wal Phillips were against it. It was certainly a big controversy that lasted quite a while.

But leg-trailing never came back, despite the demand of its enthusiastic adherents, and speedway's illustrious past had it for keeps.

Oliver Hart was generally acknowledged as the most spectacular rider in the early 'fifties, in spite of the fact that modern track conditions did not favour his amazing leg-trailing style; his riding was therefore all the more incredible. The ex-Belle Vue and Wimbledon teamster joined the Odsal team, and tearing round that vast circuit gave him an immense amount of fun and satisfaction too.

But speedway was still having a rough time and the number of tracks in operation continued to drop throughout the late 'fifties until, in 1959, there were only nine National League promotions. It was a sad state of affairs; speedway could either swing back on the up-grade or die a natural death.

But fortunately, the miracle happened. Besides a 10-team National League for 1960, a new 10-team Provincial League was instituted, and many circuits that had lain idle since the immediate post-war boom, were utilised once again. For the new group of younger promoters it was a risk, but one that eventually paid good dividends, and the Provincials flourished and flourished, while the National League promotions continued to struggle. The number, in 1964, had dwindled to seven — West Ham, Oxford, Belle Vue, Coventry, Norwich, Swindon and Wimbledon.

The Control Board then attempted to force an amalgamation of the two Leagues. But the Provincial League promoters would not agree and the 12-team set-up, Newcastle, Hackney, Sunderland, Newport, Edinburgh, Exeter, Poole, Sheffield, Middlesbrough, Cradley Heath, Long Eaton and Glasgow (finishing the League in that order) continued through the season running "black" (unlicensed), under the control of its own Association.

Many speedway riders who had hitherto enjoyed their spots of grass tracking, automatically found that they were banned from participating in the ACU grass track events and so, the Provincials, not to be out-done, staged their own! But their meetings were highly unsuccessful. Take, for instance the one organised by Charlie Foote and Mike Erskine, near Malmesbury in Wiltshire. It was a complete flop, albeit a gallant attempt in the face of forceful odds. Advertising posters of the Western Speedway Club's fixture had been torn down as were course directions signs on the actual day. But the stars of the afternoon were: Fred Powell, Bill Bridgett, Ray Harris and Peter Vandenburg.

The warring parties were certainly patriotic to their own individual causes! But a situation like this could not possibly continue and in the ensuing close season, both sides came together, amicably settling their grievances and coming up with a brave new venture — the British League — which consisted of 18 teams. The Championship was initially won by West Ham.

In 1968 came another big innovation, the British League, Division Two. Ten teams were the inaugural number, but these grew to sixteen in the following year and to seventeen in '70. And the season ended with a total of 36 teams.

Speedway was certainly back on its feet, and the increased International events had a lot to do with its renewed success. Those great Test Matches with Russia, Poland, Czechoslovakia and Sweden together with the World Team Cup competition, breathed new life into speedway. And from then on it has never looked back.

The inimitable Swedes became stronger and stronger, owing to the presence of their greatest rider, Ove Fundin. Here in England, some loved him ... some hated him, but in the end everyone was forced to acknowledge he was one of the finest riders we had ever seen. He retired from the sport with five World Championship wins under his belt, proving a supreme individual achievement.

Sponsorship — the word that has acquired a special magnetic context in speedway racing — is indeed now looked upon as a vital life-flow. And it has, undoubtedly, played a major part in speedway's re-birth. That tangible and, in some cases, considerable, backing from all kinds of business companies, has put the sport on a thorough, stabilised footing, far better than the switch-back affairs we have seen over the last four decades. And, as it enters its journey, perhaps precariously, into the latter-half of the 'seventies, we sincerely hope that its prosperity will continue.

Sponsorship of individual riders too, apart from a whole event, helps them immensely in their perennial and inevitable struggle against the ever-rising costs of spares and replacements. Sponsorship is certainly a good thing. Quite a few stadium promoters will tell you that it's not so very many years ago, when their greyhound race meetings were forced to subsidise their speedway race meetings!

Of course, the big news of 1975 was the support of a multi-thousand pound deal from Gulf Oil for the backing of the British League, Division One, and, consisting of 18 teams, was won by the all-conquering Ipswich team. Birmingham took the honours in the New National League (formerly Division Two) consisting of 20 teams.

Forceful riding by Peter Collins (left) and Martin Ashby in an England versus Sweden match during 1973

Bob Valentine's machine tries to take the upper hand as he heads Douglas Wyer, in the Yorkshire Bank Trophy contest at Sheffield in 1975

On the limit, or beyond! Chris Morton holds a slender lead over Alan Wilkinson and Carl Glover in the British World Championship Final at Coventry in 1975

Peter Collins (right) in a grand tussle with John Louis in a Belle Vue versus Ipswich match in 1975

Other big-name sponsors who serve the sport so well, and seem very satisfied with their involvement, are W.D. & H.O.Wills, through the re-named Embassy Internationale at Wimbledon which has been running for 14 seasons; the *Daily Express;* the *Sunday Mirror;* Gauloises; Golden Wonder; Favre Leuba and Marlboro. These are companies that most readily come to mind and which, in the past, have been most generous in their patronage of speedway racing.

Speedway, like time, marches on, and miraculously too, after a continuous 48 year spell ... a game surpassed for good sportsmanship, grandeur and mighty endeavour.

May its present stability and popularity continue for many ... many years.

9 The evolution of the speedway machine

For a considerable period, speedway machines have been standardised; style has been standardised too, and everything connected with a meeting is almost perfect.

But it has not always been so and many like to enjoy the pipe-dreams of the olden days, the late 'twenties and the early 'thirties, when the stars, mounted on many different makes of machines, were those who dared the most and gave the crowds the persistent thrill of the unexpected.

They were undoubtedly good times, carefree and gay, and the galaxy of models added a tremendous attraction to the whole set-up. Terrific noise seemed to add to the charm of the racing! Their variety and the ingenuity of the conversions made to them had, perhaps, a great deal to do with the rapid growth of the popularity of the sport. Speedways in their initial days were certainly paradises for motorcycle enthusiasts, for they could see almost every make of machine in action during a week's spectating.

The biggest proportion of British motorcycle manufacturers took their 350 and 500cc sports models; stripped off the lights and mudguards; fitted knee-hooks to the offside and some bracing struts on either side and advertised the machines at about £20 more than the catalogue price. How astonishing was the craze for buttressing forks and outrigging frames. The reasons seem obscure why riders and manufacturers thought this extra bracing necessary as Douglases were completely unstrutted as also was Roger Frogley's first Rudge.

Later on, appeared the American Indian machine — the only one ever to appear in speedway racing — with the formidable Art Pechar as its rider and we must not forget the famed Harley-Davidson Peashooters, neither of which carried any bracing struts whatsoever. These 345cc Peashooters were distinguished by their racing handlebars, the ends of which were almost vertical — quite the opposite of today's upright trend.

A little known fact is that the heads of the American Harley-Davidson company were none other than an Englishman, William Harley and a Scotsman, Walter Davidson!

The late 'twenties saw riders experimenting with a host of different types of machines, from OEC's with their Duplex steering to 'sloper' BSA's and from two-stroke Dunelts to James twins. No one really had an idea of what exactly was required. Several famed motorcycle manufacturers brought out impressive speedway models, highly chromed, with TT replica motors, only to see them beaten by the home-built bitzas.

In June, (1928) an Ariel captured the King's Oak one-lap record from Huxley's Douglas at over 41mph. On the same circuit Alan Day's AJS established a new 350cc lap record at 40.29mph, while Arthur Willimott won a mile scratch event at the Crystal Palace on an HRD.

Jack Parker's first race meeting was at King's Oak on Whit-Monday when he raced a 349cc BSA. Buster Frogley rode a Humber! Then a few days later, on a 346cc side-valve JAP engined Scott, Wal Phillips made a sensational debut at Stamford Bridge. A week later the same track saw its newest art. It was Art Pechar who had arrived from America. Despite a heavy fall, he pluckily broke the mile record at just under 43mph on his 350cc Indian machine, with an amazing compression ratio. Thus, another make of machine had joined the ever-growing range of dirt track models.

It was just the beginning of Pechar's rise to fame. Later in the season he made the fastest speed ever attained in Britain; he lapped the Greenford circuit at an amazing 56mph!

Eric Spencer had now started racing on A.J.Hunting's tracks, and his machine was a more carefully tuned TT Douglas. The model had a real snarl and its acceleration on the straights was terrific. Vic Huxley borrowed it one evening at Harringay and a huge chunk came off the track record.

Three riders, three styles and three roadster motorcycles! Early 1928 days at King's Oak. A.B. Duce (AJS) is followed by C. Lackford (Lackford Special) and another unidentified machine in a 500cc event

A White City favourite, Del Forster poses for a picture on an early works dirt track Rudge; this one beautifully nickel plated. Note the additional bracing struts

Frank Arthur on his Harley-Davidson "Peashooter", an American machine which would run rings around the others in the early days of British speedway
Below, A fine duel develops between a dirt track "Duggie" (left) and a Harley "Peashooter"

New rules for the control of the sport had already been made by the ACU and as the season progressed, many motorcycle manufacturers who had hitherto looked upon dirt track racing with grave disapproval, now saw that this type of racing would be a bona-fide branch of the new sport, and so became interested.

In the middle of that season there appeared a machine designed specifically for the dirt tracks by Stanley Glanfield. The new model, marketed under the name of the Glanfield Rudge Special, consisted of a 499cc Rudge Whitworth engine in a duplex frame with strutted tubes. Wheels and forks were standard Rudge fittings and the single-gear ratio was 8 to 1. The fuel tank held one gallon.

Soon after, the Rudge and AJS companies commenced building specialised models. The new AJS had a short wheelbase and the latest TT motor. It appeared firstly at the White City track at Manchester, and then in another impressive bow to the London crowds at the Crystal Palace in the hands of Roger Frogley.

The new Rudge was an all nickel-plated affair, with a standard frame incorporating triangular bracing; a special sprint tank and a sports engine.

Jim Kempster and Lionel Wills purchased one, and at the White City (London), Jim won the Silver Sash, the first time the feat had been accomplished by an Englishman in competition with the Australians on an International speedway track. "Smiling Jim" they called him, that happy-go-lucky lad from Leighton Buzzard, who at the end of the season, shared the honour with Roger Frogley of being the leading English dirt track rider. Incidentally, Jim served as First Officer in the ATA during World War Two and it's sad to relate that nearing its end, in 1945, he was killed in Germany when his plane crashed into the Rhine, and we lost one of our greatest speedway pioneers.

At Harringay there appeared Frank Arthur's new 90mph Harley, which had come straight over from the American factory. A chief point of interest was the engine's valve stems, which were little more than the thickness of an ordinary pencil. The Harley possessed fantastic acceleration and in the Silver Helmet event no other model could get anywhere near it.

A Coventry Victor machine was advertised at £85. This had a new style of frame, a short and compact one that housed its horizontal flat-twin motor. A neat and ingenious design was evolved by using a curved lower tank tube and sloping the twin saddle stays rearward, which shortened the main frame and brought the tank considerably lower.

Two other models appeared at around the same time. The single-geared P & M, the keynote of which was the simplicity in its design, and the new Zenith, a remarkable model, both for its appearance and the rigidity of its frame. The late Freddy Barnes — unfortunately killed in a German blitz on London during the war, designed the dirt track Zenith at the firm's headquarters at Hampton Court.

The Zenith's frame, practically standard, was strengthened by additional struts which in effect made it a triplex frame, the side members providing excellent protection for the engine unit. There were two models, one of 350 and the other of 500cc, both with three speeds, but single speed machines were obtainable. Several Zeniths met with immediate success. They were unlike some of its contemporaries in not being brightly plated, but nevertheless, these particular models had quite handsome appearances.

As the end of August came round, Colin Watson had a Harley Peashooter of his own and had forsaken his New Imperial. His new machine cost him £107 and the Harley riders paid 15s.7d., a gallon for the special fuel supplied by the manufacturers.

As the result of much practice work at the Greenford and White City tracks, the P & P company now offered three special speedway mounts: a 500cc model selling at 66 guineas; a two-port 350cc at 62 guineas and a 350cc single-port at 58 guineas, all with Blackburne engines. Mr. Wooler, the man in charge, devised a rear-springing system, simply as a conversion set which could be incorporated in any of the models.

On September 8, Coventry speedway had its initial glimpse of a Harley Peashooter, ridden by "Buzz" Hibberd, and in the same month the OEC company produced a speedway mount with duplex steering, the first and only machine of its kind. An experimental Royal Enfield JAP appeared, and like the majority of other makes its engine was fitted with a short length of exhaust pipe of about nine inches. The Harley and OEC machines, not forgetting that "lone" Indian of Art Pechar's, employed an even shorter length, whilst exceptions to this trend were Zenith, James and Coventry Victor, whose exhausts continued to the rear spindle.

An ACU speedway regulation, instituted later, stated that the exhaust system should extend for a minimum distance of two inches beyond the rear wheel spindle.

At the Motor Cycle Show at Olympia in November, no less than seventeen manufacturers exhibited their

A great all-rounder; Gus Kuhn is here on his Calthorpe roadster which gained a host of victories on the cinders in 1928

The dirt track Douglas ruled the roost in 1929. Here is Sydney Edmonds

Stanley Greening (left) being interviewed by the author. Stanley designed the Speedway-JAP; he put in near-on fifty years at the JAP factory ending his stint as chief technical adviser. This is 1966

dirt track models as part of their future programme, which would raise the cinder dust in 1929. The stands which displayed one or more machines were Scott, Zenith, Cotton, Royal Enfield, BSA, Dunelt, New Imperial, Chater Lea, Calthorpe, Rex Acme, Triumph, Rudge Whitworth, Douglas, New Henley, McEvoy, Coventry Victor and the James.

What a fascinating spectacle that must have been! The popularity of the show in general was emphasised by the fact that 138,417 people paid for admission.

Only two machines had really taken the limelight during the 1928 season — the Douglas and the Rudge, but the former marque had been the most popular and the most successful as the majority of the stars favoured that particular brand. It was, of course, a standard TT model, devoid of its front mudguard; its rear one cut down; the left-hand foot-rest removed; a right-hand knee-hook added and suitable controls fitted. Gear ratios were lowered by the fitting of a larger rear wheel sprocket.

The Rudge machine represented a different school of thought and the firm made their frames absolutely rigid by the addition of several struts and bracing tubes.

All the Show models, with few exceptions, were standard machines stripped and strutted, or just stripped. All carried a knee-hook and the majority had miniature fuel tanks and only a countershaft in the gear-box.

To obtain a low centre of gravity, the McEvoy model was of unusual design. It carried its 498cc single-cylinder Blackburne motor horizontally, in a special duplex frame which gave a saddle height of only 23 inches.

The new BSA model looked exceptionally neat and businesslike. It had a special frame, giving a short wheelbase, and housing a high-compression (8.5 to 1) twin-port 493cc engine. The oil system was a simple hand pump in the top of the petrol/oil tank. Transmission was through an ordinary BSA clutch and gearbox, but there were no intermediate pinions or a kickstart. A variety of sprockets were provided for use on different-sized tracks; a large gauze cinder shield covered the whole engine and longer life to the motor was ensured by an air-cleaner on the racing type carburettor. Optional size beaded-edge tyres were fitted, but the tread was quite standard.

Incidentally, before the BSA speedway models left the factory, each one was tested by Jack Parker on a new track which the company had constructed at its works!

The Scott manufacturers employed an open frame, a TT engine, and the heart rending yowl of this motor was terrifically exciting. The model had a 3-speed gearbox, specially braced Scott forks of the old type, a smaller-than-standard radiator and a neat exhaust system.

One of the best ideas however, for protection of the working parts from cinder dust, appeared on the Rex Acme. The engine was totally enclosed in metal gauze reaching to the cylinder base and extending underneath the crankcase, totally enclosing, amongst other things, the primary chain.

On the Triumph machine there were two rear wheel sprockets of different size, one on each side of the hub. The wheel, quickly detachable and adjustable, could be taken out and reversed in a matter of seconds which gave the choice of two gear ratios.

The Royal Enfield and Calthorpe manufacturers, favoured the Rudge method of bracing their standard frames, whilst New Imperial went one step further with a veritable nest of tubes, one of which had to be removed before even the plug could be extracted! Even the wheels carried extra spokes, strung tennis-racket fashion, direct from one side of the rim to the other.

The James concern employed the new 496cc V-twin, ohv engine in their models, and on the Calthorpe stand appeared Jack Martin. He was the unfortunate fellow who lay unconscious for 21 days following a nasty crash at Stamford Bridge earlier in the season; an accident which caused his retirement from the sport.

The prices of these various speedway mounts are interesting. The Rudge and BSA models with specially-tuned engines were listed at £70 each which, even in those far-off days, was considered reasonable. The Douglas with a TT engine had always been higher in price at £85. The firm's stand was the meeting-place for all the elite of the dirt track world. "Sprouts" Elder, Roger Frogley and various promoters and a host of others were all there and Freddie Dixon and Rex Judd were talking "dirt" by the hour! These were, of course, the official Douglas tuners.

With "Show time" over the 1929 dirt track season soon came round and practising was in full swing at the White City (London) track as early as the first week in March. It was immediately obvious that an enormous variety of machines would still be ridden. Nick Nicol rode the bends nearly flat-out on a Scott; Mart Seiffert performed on a BSA; Bill Crouch showed great promise on an AJS, while Jimmy Stevens who raced a private Norton at King's Oak the previous year, was really tearing around on a Duggie.

Frank Arthur, rode his brand new 500cc Harley-Davidson, which he was running-in. This particular machine

Top, *One of the three-hundred speedway machines built by Comerfords Limited in the 1930s*
Centre, *Wal Phillips, idol of the Stamford Bridge crowds, on one of the very first JAP-engined machines in 1930*

Colin Watson, the Wembley Lions captain, in 1931 on his famous Harley-JAP which held the National quarter-mile record, the Crystal Palace track record and the Wimbledon Track Championship

was an exact replica of the now famous 350cc Harley Peashooter except, of course, that the bore was a little larger. Only three pounds constituted the difference in the weight of the two models.

In the same month, a craftsman's handiwork appeared at the White City. It was the new dirt track Wallis, designed and built by George Wallis. The model had special lugs which had been designed for the chain stays to prevent rear-frame whip, and therefore minimised chain breakage; duplex lower tank rails were employed to give added rigidity; the front down tube was slightly more curved to bring the engine further forward; the countershaft was fixed and ran on roller-bearings; the front forks, to prevent twisting, were incorporated with a special arrangement of shock dampers. Almost any engine could be fitted, either 350 or 500cc.

Frank Arthur took the Wallis, installed with a 344cc racing JAP engine, round for a few laps and pronounced it one of the finest machines he had ever ridden. He said it really steered itself over the bumps.

An entirely new redesigned Scott was available at £95 and had been selected, among others, by Arthur Franklyn, Frank Varey, Wilf McClure and Oliver Langton.

The end of April saw the new dirt track Wallis being manufactured by Comerford's Motor Exchange of Thames Ditton. In the ensuing month Colin Watson on his 350cc Harley Peashooter (the same machine on which Frank Arthur had so successfully performed the previous season), raised the Stamford Bridge record to 46.87mph.

Frank Varey rose to stardom rapidly on his Scott at the beginning of the season and was now one of the most successful riders in the North at his home track, Belle Vue.

Art Pechar, "Silent Art" they called him, was again racing in England on his roaring Indian, but he was only a shadow of his former self. That accident at the White City in 1928 was a bad one, when he dived headlong into the fence, in a challenge race with Billy Lamont, which put him out of action for a month. He was near to breaking his neck on this occasion. Then came another serious spill at the start of the '29 season, also at the White City, in which he suffered an injured shoulder and a broken ankle.

It was obvious that these two crashes had some effect on the famous American, who had caused such a sensation the previous year, and Art and his lone Indian returned to their native country for good. Another page of speedway's history had been written.

Billy Lamont's form at West Ham early in May, (1929) was reminiscent of his riding at the opening Stamford Bridge meeting, namely, nearly flat-out all the way; no one could get anywhere near him, as his AJS was now powered by one of the new overhead-camshaft TT engines and the power unit had terrifically high revolutions.

Frank Varey, now employed at the Scott works in the experimental department, had already beaten the redoubtable Arthur Franklyn at Belle Vue, and in recent meetings had acquired a Silver Helmet, a Golden Gauntlet, various Trophies and, at Warrington, a Golden Helmet.

Eric Langton, although usually Rudge mounted, appeared on a Scott at Leeds in May, and this month also saw the opening, on Whit Saturday, of Britain's first third of a mile track, the Leicester Super, when "Sprouts" Elder (Douglas) clocked the fastest time of day at just over 47mph.

At that magnificent circuit the Douglases wound up to a scream that was never heard on the smaller circuits, and when the top-notchers went into the bends at close on 60mph they provided a real sight.

Later Jack Chapman lapped the same track at over 49mph, while at the Crystal Palace the flying-mile record was gained by Triss Sharp and his Duggie at 44.68mph. He also equalled Ron Johnson's flying-start lap record of 45.45mph.

The middle of the season saw the appearance of the new Coventry Victor dirt track model fitted with a 488cc ohv, flat-twin engine and shortly afterwards, Arthur Jervis the White City (Manchester) Captain rode a special Rudge, while Roger Frogley appeared at Stamford Bridge on a new Harley. Later Roger won the Star Championship.

At Exeter speedway there appeared two Velocettes, works models, which looked very neat and efficient.

In the North, Eric Langton and his home-built Rudge were going great guns. Here is one of his week's achievements. Monday: a first-class win at Warrington and another at Liverpool. Tuesday: broke three records at Leeds. Wednesday: broke the Belle Vue track record twice and won the Golden Helmet. Thursday: three firsts at Liverpool. Friday: three firsts at Newcastle. Saturday: three firsts at Leeds and the track record beaten.

Wembley's £200 meeting attracted a crowd of 41,000. Jim Kempster broke Wimbledon's record on his Rudge. No longer was his machine strutted up generally, and the standard frame had been slightly modified to give a different steering angle; the forks had been replaced by American-style Webb forks, identical to those fitted to the dirt track Velocettes. The result was a machine with wonderful track-holding qualities.

Colin Ford rode a Wallis while Max Grosskreutz had a Harley with an AJS motor; two really hot machines. With various other models coming into the limelight, the sport was taking on a definite machine interest in addition to the purely rider side of the question.

As the season drew to a close, Frank Arthur was riding a Rudge-engined Wallis; Wal Phillips a Douglas with Jack Parker also Douglas-mounted. Wal raised the Stamford Bridge flying-mile record to over 45mph, while Syd Jackson on a Rudge raised the same record at the Leicester Super to just under 50mph!

The quantity of dirt track specials exhibited by manufacturers at the 1930 Motorcycle Show at Olympia was smaller than that of the previous year but the quality distinctively better. Another dirt track machine appeared for the first time. It was the Sunbeam which had several very good features. The lowest-priced dirt track model however, was the New Hudson at £59, with an all chromium finish. A bright finish certainly counted on the tracks, as the speedway public loved colour and noise.

The ordinary dirt track Douglas motor developed on an average about 27 brake horse-power (on petrol-benzole mixture) when it left the works. For an extra £10, any rider could obtain a supertuned engine which would add at least another 5 bhp. The work was carried out personally by Freddie Dixon and Rex Judd, both of whom have now sadly passed on.

During that 1929 season the Douglas firm had sold about 1,300 dirt track models, which constituted a remarkable record. Johnnie Hoskins asked the company to turn him out machines that made as fiendish a din as possible and also, if it was possible, a spot of fire-breathing apparatus in the exhaust system would be welcomed!

Truly remarkable to an impressive degree was the Company's complete domination of the British, Australian, European and South American cinder circuits, which varied from around 380 yards per lap to a third of a mile. The Douglas models used in Britain by the Australian vanguard of powerslide practitioners were built with a frame made up of a front section of the RA machine and the back section of the OC. As soon as these machines had demonstrated their superiority over the be-strutted singles that were the contemporary British idea of a dirt track bike, Douglas Motors Ltd., immediately got to work and put two cinder-trackers into production. These, named the DT5 and DT6, were identical in every way except their engine capacity, 500 and 600cc respectively. The price, brand new, as they went on to the market? £85 and £90.

Nothing could live with the fabulous dirt Duggies; they were the tracks' ideal machine; they not only out-accelerated everything else in sight, but they handled on the loose surfaces with inimitable surefootedness and controllability. So dirt track aspirants to fame and fortune rushed to the Kingswood (Bristol) factory's racing offices ... with ready cash.

Although the Douglas firm spread its wings much further than its rivals, the Company was by no means the only marque in Britain that carved for itself a permanent niche in the history of speedway racing.

Rudge Whitworth, with their 100mph Ulster engine, obtained at least 30bhp and could turn out such motors in unlimited quantities. Freddie Dixon promised 34bhp with his supertuning on the 1930 special Douglas motor, and with the Rudge some great dirt track battles were certainly in the offing.

The Rudge was almost identical to those that appeared towards the end of the 1928 season, developed from experiment and experience of Jim Kempster and Arthur Jervis, although its frame was no longer strutted.

However the 1929 season had left no doubt that the Douglas was still by far the most popular and most successful dirt track machine. Apart from actual race results, the fact that it was possible to attend a meeting and see nothing but Douglases really proved the point.

One thing for 1930 was certain. The battle for supremacy would be a titanic struggle among the various manufacturers, which could only result in racing of a higher standard than anything yet seen. The real battle would undoubtedly be between the Douglas and the Rudge, both of which had undisputed sway. Although as far as design went, they were poles apart, but they had one thing in common — tremendously fast motors.

And yet another famous motorcycle manufacturer entered the dirt track sphere, with special works models. It was the Norton company, but only a small number of these machines were manufactured, and the majority went to Australia. In England, Eric Langton and Ron Johnson had a period Norton-mounted and Stan Catlett too, that voluble little Australian who was riding for Wembley.

The Norton dirt track machine's general appearance was superb, and it was a matter of some surprise that the famous firm did not cling more tenaciously to the rapidly growing market, although, of course, its activities in road racing probably precluded this.

As early as April, (1930) it could be seen that the latest Rudge was fast coming into popular favour. One of

Billy Lamont with his 1931 works Rudge. These machines were ridden almost exclusively in that season

these motors had been installed in Colin Watson's Harley. Billy Lamont, on a Rudge, became the first rider to lap the Wembley circuit at over 40mph, and it was reported that in his record-breaking ride his handlebars were less than a foot from the cinders!

The whole of the Crystal Palace team consisting of Triss Sharp (Captain), Ron Johnson, Harry Shepherd, Clem Mitchell, Wally Lloyd, Joe Francis and Roger Frogley were now riding Rudge machines, although Len Parker (Wimbledon) still remained true to his Douglas.

The Association of Motorcycle Track Racing Promoters then issued a statement. It requested that in advertisements or any other matter relating to speedway racing the word speedway should be used in place of dirt track.

You will have seen however, that gradually the development of the speedway machine had stabilised itself into two schools of thought. There were those riders who held that the long wheelbase, smooth traction attributes of the Bristol-born blue and silver twin gave real broadsiding, while there were others who favoured the short, vertical Rudge single.

By the middle of the season the speedway Rudge appeared to have established a definite superiority, although it was well to remember that sheer speed was not the only deciding factor in a race.

Riders were still experimenting with frames. They put engines forward, backward, high and low. And saddles too. Front forks were to be seen at all angles; hacksaws and brazing kits worked overtime.

Although the new Rudge was causing a general changeover, the fabulous Duggie had been a turn on its own. Frequently it unsaddled its rider to jump and race along on its own.

An amusing incident occurred at the Cleveland Park circuit at Middlesbrough in 1928. Ron Johnson provided the 12,000 crowd with the thrill of their lives. Riding his Douglas flat-out in an endeavour to overtake Fred Creasor (Rudge) the two machines touched and Ron took a spectacular toss, sliding yards on his back and somersaulting twice. But the remarkable thing about the crash was that his machine, after being flat on the ground, suddenly rose on its wheels again and set off at full speed round the track! Riderless, it actually overtook Creasor and then again the two machines came into contact. This time the Douglas shot off at a tangent, cleared the safety-fence, and landed with a terrific crash on the second fence, where it came to rest within a few feet of the massed spectators. Fred Creasor also came off, but neither he nor Johnson were hurt.

The Douglas, which undoubtedly provides some of speedway's richest memories, had, of course, always been the crowd's favourite, for its noise and spectacular broadsiding ability made it loved by all. But for easy maintenance, riders now preferred the Rudge single. Even today, and I'm certainly no exception, many believe that much of the gripping thrill of dirt track racing was lost when the real leg-trailing broadsiders relinquished their Bristol-born twins in favour of the less spectacular singles.

But time marches on ... with the changing of many scenes and the world famous dirt Duggies, machines that had previously been the cat's whisker, began a downward slide and a new machine era started.

Towards the end of that 1930 season came the first signs of yet another revolution. Prior to this time, Messrs.J.A.Prestwich had not concerned themselves very much with speedway racing, but Stanley Greening and Wal Phillips, who was also an employee of the JAP factory in North London, produced a new racing motor. The speedway JAP, and later an assortment of JAP-powered singles, permanently forced the Kingswood breed off the sunny side of the street. And so, the Golden Days of the speedway Douglas sadly came to an end. But those snarling, fiery low-slung twins, the real thrill-makers of the tracks, that made many a pioneer famous, have always been affectionately remembered by everyone who saw them in action ... blazing the speedway trail.

I'm glad I was in at the beginning of British broadsiding — if only as a schoolboy!

The light JAP engine was mounted in a Comerford Wallis frame assembly and Wal Phillips made a spectacular debut in early August, (1930) at Stamford Bridge with the new model. He won the Stamford Bridge Championship Riband and in a whirlwind ride he clocked a record of over 46mph. This clearly showed that the JAP engine was the most efficient one yet produced for its particular purpose. Stamford Bridge therefore, by Wal's amazing effort, secured the title of the fastest ¼-mile track in the country and his speed also constituted a British and European Mile Speedway record. However, in October Wal bettered his own record, turning the 440 yard circuit in 18.8secs. — 47.87mph!

The JAP motor dropped very conveniently into short wheel-base frames, like that of the Rudge, and lent themselves to a less spectacular but more effective technique of broadsiding, close to the white line, with a minimal angle of corrective lock. Shortest time around the tracks decided what won and what lost races, and the singles, in the unarguable language of the timekeepers stop watches, made the fastest times.

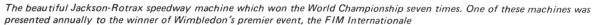

The beautiful Jackson-Rotrax speedway machine which won the World Championship seven times. One of these machines was presented annually to the winner of Wimbledon's premier event, the FIM Internationale

From then on it was a JAP engine in a 'something' frame for practically every rider and amazingly, after 46 years, the same set-up, but to a lesser degree, continues today with many riders.

That universal adoption, albeit a creditable adoption, seemed to be the first step in standardisation which we are still faced with today — with the Jawa, the sport having become far too stereotyped. Nowadays, and for a considerable time too, there has been little to choose in outward appearance between one machine and another, apart from perhaps, colour schemes. Different makes of speedway machines certainly add extra glamour to racing, and apart from creating additional competitiveness, entertainment value is greatly increased.

The first Eso speedway model to be seen in Britain appeared in the hands of that magnificent Swedish ace, Ove Fundin in early 1961. The Czech company gave him one, but he rode his JAP engined machine in all the important events.

Alec Jackson Exports Ltd., in North London however, became the original UK distributor of Eso motors in 1965, but the following year, Barry Briggs became the sole UK concessionaire at his Southampton premises for the complete Eso (or Jawa machine as it is now called).

As rider-agent, Barry came into a load of teething troubles, but later, as these were overcome, he brilliantly demonstrated the machine's capabilities in no uncertain manner, and today, about 80% of riders use them. But, as the British Weslake gets into its stride, the percentage could be on the downward turn in 1976!

Then, of course, there was the beautifully-built Jackson Rotrax JAP, winner of the World Championship seven times. A magnificent machine in every respect and one that is still produced today under George Greenwood's banner. But it is one from a pattern that has become standardised in the same way that the whole sport has become moulded into a single form.

Committed to a rigid programme with a practically unvariable team and a pit full of machines, as alike as peas in a pod, there is little opportunity for promoters to provide variety in speedway today. Neither for all the various developments, etc., is there much improvement in the spectacle. It is certainly an amazing fact that speeds are only slightly faster than they were 47 years ago by just a few mph! The foot-forward style of riding, close to the white line, has robbed the enthusiasts of their one-time thrill, that full lock wide and wild technique, while payments on results in terms of points rather than on a Sprouts Elder-like ability to entertain to an impressively high degree, are all factors that have tended to kill the big thrills that the old-timers so gallantly gave, and so sadly seek to recapture.

But I suppose, as it must be with all things ... time still marches on. From its rough-and-tumble beginning, speedway racing has sorted itself out, to become a highly-orgainsed sporting attraction that claims the second largest spectator sport in the country. Of its popularity, there is certainly no doubt!

10 Speedway engines

Think a moment ... and you'll be sure to agree it's amazing fact that an engine which began life in August, 1930, should still be manufactured today, after an unbroken run of over four decades. That's the incredible British-made 497cc speedway JAP.

Admittedly, in speedway, the Czechoslovakian-built Jawa has broken the long-held monopoly of the speedway JAP, but, be it in speedway, grass, sand, or ice racing, there's plenty of dynamite in the old JAP yet!

For this single power unit to completely dominate its own particular corner of the sport for 35 years is incredible enough, but to do so without any significant change in design, makes it that much more a super achievement. No other engine in the world can touch its longevity record; all the others lag far, far behind. Another of J. A. Prestwich's countless records is that, at one time, every rider in the world was JAP-engined mounted, which is really astounding.

Like Brittania ruling the waves, so the JAP motor ruled speedway. No one else produced anything equable, in fact, no one even tried, not until 35 years later! But why today, you might ask, are 80-per-cent of riders using Jawa engines? Nelson Harring, the renowned Somerset tuner gives his answer: "It is simply because the Jawa is a complete speedway machine in itself, and, as such, is an extremely easy model to ride. Another contributing factor, is, perhaps, that the unit needs less maintenance than the JAP."

"But the Jawa motor is not problem free," he adds with a smile.

It is not surprising that the Iron Curtain Jawa firm found it a long hard struggle to emulate the all-conquering JAP. In fact its engine is really a refined copy of the basic JAP conception. The Eso, as it was called originally, means Ace and incidentally, the first model to be seen in Britain, appeared in the hands of Ove Fundin, who had previously raced one at Rowley Park, Australia in 1961. Quiet man Ove was the one who shrewdly and wisely switched from an Eso to a JAP-engined machine, to win the 1967 World Championship at Wembley.

An all-alloy engine with the rocker-gear and pushrods completely enclosed, the purpose-built Jawa churns out around 54bhp at 7,000rpm but can safely be taken up to 8,000. Like the JAP it is relatively a light, big single, with magneto ignition, a total-loss oil system, part-spherical cylinder head and high-dome piston. Its bore and stroke is 88mm x 82mm. As the motor thrives on revs., it favours the full-throttle lads.

The JAP motor has, not surprisingly, been copied abroad by other firms, as in the case of the Polish FIZ engine which, like the others, automatically pays the JAP Company a great compliment.

Petrol — forsaken in 1929 — is never used as fuel and methanol has taken its place. Consumed at a rate of about six miles per gallon, this special fuel makes the JAP or the Jawa a very thirsty motor. Incidentally, the rules forbid any additive like nitro, which is strictly banned.

The former Company of Alec Jackson Ltd., in Northern London (now taken over by ex-rider George Greenwood) was the original UK distributor of Eso engines in 1965, but in the following year, Barry Briggs became the sole UK concessionaire for the complete Eso machine.

In '65, we saw the Emmott Matchless speedway engine and a few months after came the Greeves two-stroke, to be followed, in '68, by the Hedlund from Sweden — a twin overhead-camshaft motor. The latter two were tested out by the Hackney star, Bengt Jansson.

A year later came the MS, an Australian motor manufactured by Brisbane-dealer, Clarie Meirson, weighing ten pounds less than the JAP. This was followed by the SO engine — a product of Japan's Aircraft Corporation.

Then came, in 1970, to challenge the JAP and Jawa monopoly, the beautifully produced Cole motor,

The amazing JAP engine manufactured for an incredible run of over 45 years — perhaps that is a record in itself

The British Weslake engine, pioneered by John Louis

designed by ex-rider Howard Cole ... and his innovative father. The Cole engine had cost over £30,000! and that included £10,000 for tooling up. In grass track racing it has achieved some magnificent honours.

Fred Jolly, the Beaumont (South Australia) agent, spent a small fortune during the five years he took in producing his SR60 in '72 — an engine called the Southern Racer, which developed 60bhp!

A year later the BSA engine had arrived on the English scene, based on the firm's illustrious motocross unit. This speedway prototype was tested by Nigel Boocock, on one occasion in a 100-lap stint at Brandon. The project, however, was aimed at filling the gap created by the boom in speedway racing, and the acute shortage of JAP and Jawa motors ... but, for the Company, serious financial problems lay ahead.

More recently comes Ronnie Moore, twice World Champion, who, until his serious crash, had been experimenting at his Christchurch (NZ) agency with a speedway Kawasaki. He was also helping the Benelli firm in Italy to develop its own speedway engine.

However, all these various engines, good as they undoubtedly were, proved not quite good enough for top speedway racing and they made no significant impact. One by one, for one reason or another, they fell quietly by the wayside.

The ESO engine pictured here in a complete machine and now called the Jawa is manufactured in Czechoslovakia

The only engine to have immediate success almost on its initiation is the fabulous 1975 British Weslake, a beautiful four-valver. Machine-wise, it's the most exciting mechanical development for a decade.

Already proving the Jawa's most serious rival, the engine really came into its own in the British Speedway Final when John Louis (the winner), Peter Collins 2nd, Ray Wilson 4th, and Martin Ashby 5th, were Weslake mounted. And this magnificent achievement came only nine months after the first prototype caused such a sensation at the Lydden circuit, in Kent.

As well as a Weslake-engined machine taking third spot in the World Final, ridden by "Tiger" Louis (the first Englishman to finish in the first three since 1962), this particular motor achieved other notable successes.

With the Weslake motor itself; Neil Street's 4-valve conversion; Sweden's 4-valve ERM and the Weslake JAP or Jawa 4-valve RL conversion sets, handled by Reg Luckhurst (Wimbledon's eight-year teamster) as the sole agent, four-valve domination of speedway may be complete as the '76 season ends. Then the sport will have turned a complete circle!

It may surprise you to know that "four-valvers" are nothing new in speedway. Back in the late 'twenties and early 'thirties, the famous works Rudge Whitworths all had four-valve motors. In fact in 1930 they had already proved their worth, so forthrightly evidenced as practically every rider of note in the country was Rudge mounted. And at that particular time, Vic Huxley was running no fewer than five speedway Rudges! Incidentally, one of the few now remaining is owned by Bob Jones, chief mechanic at Blunsdon, who has an identical model.

Machine-wise it's an exciting era, and the new Weslake could make the mighty Jawa an also ran. That's the probable message from its performance so far.

Today a new modern speedway engine costs around half a thousand pounds, seven times more than a COMPLETE SPEEDWAY MACHINE cost in 1930!

Patriotic Ray Wilson, one of our greatest sportsmen, says: "The Weslake Company is to be congratulated in putting an engine into real competitive position and I'm proud to be riding with one of the firm's motors. I'm glad to see "Buy British" as one of speedway's slogans."

And patriotism is certainly an admirable trait.

11 The Unsung heroes

In speedway racing, as in all other sports, it is the man in the public eye that receives all the adulation of the crowd. Although every rider appreciates his own popularity as an indication of his success, he himself gives much of the credit to his mechanic or tuner.

The workshop mechanics are the back room boys of speedway racing and their skill and workmanship is quickly indicated by the performance of their riders. Two highly skilled tuners that immediately come to mind are Nelson Harring and Bob Jones, who live and talk little else than speedway engines. Then there was the notable Alfred Cole who alas, is no longer with us. There are others, of course, up and down the country.

It is only natural that the thousands of enthusiasts who visit the various circuits to cheer their favourite riders should be interested only in their own particular heroes; after all, to them it is only the man in the saddle that matters. But one would hate to think what kind of racing we should have without the "Invisible Man" or, in other words, the Tuner. As vital to the game as the riders themselves, his work can be equally exacting.

No tuner is alone responsible for a Championship victory. Similarly, the rider who ultimately takes the title cannot take all the credit. The accolade is jointly, and collectively, to the tuner and rider together.

The racing motor has a tremendous task in life. It must start readily, accelerate like a rocket, and be absolutely reliable. With the present high-speed engines, races are virtually won and lost in the workshop.

Concealed neatly away on the tree-clad slopes of the Frome Valley, near Freshford, in Somerset, and only a stone's throw from the celebrated Iford Manor and its beautiful Italian Gardens, lies the residence of Nelson Harring. Fastened to an iron gate, a tiny name-plate marked "Silver Birches" offers the only clue as to his whereabouts, for the roof of his house is lower than the road!

The tuning workshops, where the urge for so many ultra-fast machines is produced, nestles snugly alongside the house, which is actually built on to a face of solid rock. An extremely secluded, but glorious spot, for Nelson and his wife love the quiet life.

I would not be surprised if there are some who would probably say; "Who is this man, Nelson Harring?", for a more serious "hide his light under a bushel" fellow would be difficult to find. He is really many things. First and foremost he is an engineer, and a talented one too. He is a tuner of racing engines and his reputation stands as high as anyone's and higher than most. He is one of the few specialists today who can lay claim to associations with the motorcycle sport for over forty years, with successes far too numerous to enumerate.

It all began early in 1930 when, as a young lad, he started in earnest his engineering apprenticeship. Later he became friendly with an established tuner, Richard Chapman and also another engineer, the late George Thatcher, who was described as a magnificent designer and an engineering genius.

And so, as the years went by, with two superb tutors, Nelson Harring's climb to fame was perhaps inevitable. He developed into a most painstaking, thorough and brilliant tuning specialist.

Linking up with Mike Erskine, then riding in the Bristol speedway team, in the immediate pre-war years, Nelson worked on the Southampton team's motors and those of many other leading riders as he still does. He also tuned for the famous American brothers, Jack and Cordy Milne.

Nelson Harring's engineering and tuning activities came to a sudden, compulsory standstill which the Second World War was to extend along the years, but rather than cooling down, his passion smouldered and eventually exploded with renewed vigour. This was in 1946.

With the war in the background, grass track and speedway racing headed towards their biggest-ever boom and, of course, Nelson was inundated with work. It was big-time racing ... and certainly big time tuning. A queue of cars often formed on the road above his workshops ... a batch of riders had come to collect their highly-tuned motors ... some had come for advice, whilst others unloaded their engines. Despite the constant pressure, our racing specialist always had a patient ear, as, of course, he still has, for any rider's problems.

I looked him up one recent afternoon. To be attended to were a dozen or so JAP and Eso motors plus a few scramble engines. Nelson endeavoured to explain the intricacies of several motors, and my non-mechanical mind wrestled desperately with the technical jargon which was affectionately and eloquently recited for my benefit. But my brain refused to register. Nevertheless, my eyes were more helpful. They decided that Nelson Harring was something of a genius with engines, many of which bore a tagged label. These were ready for collection; beautifully prepared, they glistened in the light.

Always shunning the limelight, this speedway and grass track engine tuner, is an out-and-out craftsman, who is pretty certain to be able to lift the power curve of any motor, simply by careful tuning. His skill and painstaking attention to tiring detail provide a tremendous fillip to the sport; his innumerable successes make opponents ride harder, more clever, chasing always the elusive honour of defeating his super-tuned engines.

Essentially an individualist; an introvert too; tuning to him is a job that he settles down to in a very conscientious manner, and the thought of self-glorification is so very far away. Sincerity, veracity, enormous humility and obvious ability, are the virtues that took Nelson to the top. In friendship he is warm-hearted and spirited; in business he is exactly the same.

But his success is due primarily to his natural ability, dauntless determination and unquestioned courage. He rose to fame through hard work, brain and brilliance. Precise in his work; untemperamental; he has but one objective, to get the very best from every engine.

Nelson Harring's well-equipped workshops, crammed with various machinery, odd-shaped pistons, special valves and fine precision tools, is always a place of memories, anticipation and experiment. Busy it always is, often far into the early hours of many mornings, for Nelson is really a motorcycle scientist with his own ideas. He even manufactures his own cams, crankcase liners, con-rods, flywheel assemblies and a host of other accessories; in fact he designs and makes most of his tools, jigs, fixtures and such machines as cam milling and grinding equipment.

To many speedway enthusiasts, a tuning depot may conjure up the sound of revving motors and high-pitched engines; a noisy place in every sense of the word. But not so at the Harring premises. It's exactly the opposite.

When Nelson has tuned an engine it isn't run afterwards for testing. In fact, normally it doesn't fire before it reaches the track; clear evidence of the confidence that so many riders place in him ... clear evidence why the "Silver Birches" estate, for it comprises four acres, is so peaceful.

Now sadly passed on, the great Freddie Dixon — famous rider, driver and factory tuner of the dirt track Douglases in speedway's early days — once remarked that he was amazed that Nelson Harring could tune an engine without afterwards finishing the job with a test. Speedwayman Maury Mattingly took his Harring-tuned machines all the way to race in Venezuela several years ago, without previously running them!

And so, as my story unfolds, it becomes clearer what a remarkable fellow is this man Harring.

Decorating one of the walls of his spacious lounge, hangs a large and beautiful oil painting, a portrait of Mabel, his wife, which testifies in no uncertain manner his skill as an artist. Besides Nelson's artistic tendencies he is very interested in the Law, and Human Rights are often a topicality.

I took stock of the wall decor in one workshop. Who but the hardest boiled of humans could contemplate that fond array of souvenirs without a nostalgic pang ... a framed photograph of Eric Fernihough in 1935, astride Britain's fastest motorcycle, the thousand Brough JAP, with its speedway barrels, etc., ... a picture of a Houtman car with a wooden chassis that Nelson used to drive ... another of the 1948 Bristol Bulldog speedway team with that beautiful live bulldog squatting down with the riders in the front row and thoroughly enjoying itself ... a telegram from Fred Tuck after winning the World Championship round at Bristol in 1949 which read: "Wonderful motor — thanks a million — Fred." And to come to more recent years, a large German poster advertising one of the Osnabruck International meetings in which Lew Coffin was destined to appear as one of the top stars.

Thinking out new methods of gaining more power from his clients' motors is an ever-present thought for Nelson, but it is obvious he holds many "wrinkles." He tuned for the majority of the Bristol speedway team which swallowed up many of his patient hours and their rise to First Division racing in 1950 can certainly be attributed to his superior work, which remained in evidence until the track closed in 1960.

I asked Nelson Harring for his assessment of just a few of "his" riders: "Billy Hole, the Bristol skipper, was

In the warm summer days, tuning ace Nelson Harring, prefers to work on his terrace. Yet another JAP engine is about to be dismantled

not only an outstanding rider but a terrific character off the track with his gay personality. He once gained 22 successive maximums which I think was a record. Then there was the gallant Eric Salmon who broke the Knowle track record more times than I can remember. Dick Bradley was another Bulldog who didn't bother to run his motors until he reached the track. I tuned for him for 16 years and apart from his terrific riding ability, he was a wonderful example of a business-like fellow as well as one of the highest average point scorers. Chris Blewett seemed to me a real gentleman who was so appreciative of my work for many years. I rate Tim Bungay as one of the bravest fellows that speedway has ever seen; he was not afraid to ride anything, even after a terrible crash at Exeter. Then, to come up to more recent times there is Richard May, a brilliant rider, and young John Davis, who seems assured of a great future."

Amongst a host of other riders, Nelson has tuned for Neil Street, the Rogers Brothers and Ove Fundin. With Mike Erskine, they tuned the Southampton and Harringay team's motors in the late 'thirties, together with the American team's engines, the top boys of this contingent being Jack and Cordy Milne, and the late Wilbur Lamoreaux.

Essentially a fundamentalist with a down-to-earth appreciation of the importance of engine preparation, Nelson Harring's life-time of accumulated knowledge is readily offered to any rider. He has achieved an enviable reputation and as speedway and grass track "horses" are his ruling passion, the motors that are entrusted to him, after the usual doctoring, possess that little extra something and that's exactly what counts in racing today.

This master-tuner who works so silently "behind the scenes", avoids publicity like the plague. In fact he is probably one of the least known of the accepted aces of the tuning world. Perhaps one reason is that he rarely attends a race meeting.

Full of new ideas, Nelson's only trouble is that 24 hours a day is just not enough. Work continually keeps coming in and he is perennially behind schedule.

Preparing racing engines is, at times, a hectic and trying business. During the season, while most of us sleep, this "Man of Power" maintains an unrelentless effort to keep his boys happy in their non-stop racing programme.

It is little wonder therefore, that a man who is so industrious and so methodical in all he does, should have achieved success in sports for which he has such a natural aptitude. Allied to these useful qualities is a determination which enables him to hold his own in any circumstance.

Yet with all his attributes and monumental successes, he cloaks his vast mechanical knowledge under a disarming smile of extreme modesty.

Wearing a cap, a cravat and high-necked pullover, etc., a short, stocky figure is sometimes seen walking in the lonely, but picturesque lanes around Iford, and obviously admiring the scenery. A far cry from the noise and excitement of the racing circuits or the exacting demands of a top flight tuner's bench. Yet this is how The Mechanical Man snatches a few minutes relaxation, away from a world in which the famous British JAP engine and the Jawa fills almost the whole picture.

The speedway and grass track stars, riding Harring-tuned machinery could not and cannot, achieve such top-notch successes as they have, without a super-tuned engine. Such honours underline forcibly the technical ingenuity of the Somerset veteran. Scarcely a star has twinkled in the Southern grass track and speedway firmament that has not owed something to this man's mechanical mind.

Precisely what is the HARRING TOUCH? Well, it really boils down to an infinite capacity for taking pains, based of course, on a genuine love of his work. The sort of love that made him, in the distant past, decide to make engine tuning a full-time occupation which replaced far more lucrative employment and the sort of love that often takes him partially through the night in finishing a particular motor.

So much for Harring the Tuner. What of Nelson the man? He is a very reticent kind of fellow, but he freely parts with any technical advice to the beginner or the expert too; he is, I think, the embodiment of the schoolboy's impression of a Tuner. He is short, and has a slight stoop. His voice is quiet and well modulated; his hair is grey and parted from a high forehead; round-faced, with a thick but neatly-trimmed moustache, his eyes are keen, lively, inquisitive perhaps, above all else.

Quiet and self-effacing? That assessment well applies to him also, but he has something else, an engaging manner which goes straight to the hearts of riders and friends alike. It could be, of course, that his extremely placid nature comes from living in the very heart of the country, far away from the hustle and bustle of today's city and town life, which he thoroughly dislikes.

Any man, like NELSON HARRING, who puts more into anything than he takes out, is to be highly commended.

I admire him greatly.

The poster read; "Grass Track Racing: Trowbridge, Wilts., June 25, 1932." It was a must for me, and that sunny afternoon I saw Jack Dale of Warminster emerge as the star of the afternoon with two firsts, two seconds, a third and the fastest time of day.

But there was a young lad, no more than twenty-years-old, who, on a "499" Rudge performed with distinction. In the 500cc ohv and unlimited cc events he gained victories in both his heats and also a second in the Final of the former event. I mentally marked him as a youngster with a bright future.

A year later however, at the same venue I watched the same lad racing again and he took the place of Jack Dale as the star rider. After clocking a heat and final win in the unlimited cc race, he won the premier event — the Six Fastest Riders' race in an exciting tussle with George Butcher and Geoff Sleightholme.

The boy was, of course, MIKE ERSKINE, the Etonian, who was destined to reach the speedway heights some seventeen years later and to produce the famous "Staride" frame. Today, and for a considerable number of years previous, he is acknowledged as one of the country's greatest engine tuners.

Incidentally, Reg Robins — later an Exeter notability — rode at that same meeting with a 494cc Douglas and a 349cc Harley-Davidson, the latter being probably the only machine of its kind ever seen in grass track racing.

Three riders of the Brandon Club had shown abundant promise at Coventry speedway in 1933, and George O'Brien, Les Wheeler, and Mike Erskine were the boys in question.

It had however, always been the policy of Fred Mockford to encourage new talent, and in May, 1934, he signed all three juniors. At that particular time, New Cross had two speedway teams, one in Division One and the other in the Second Division. Mike was appointed captain of the latter. He remained with the team for a further season and, after a spell with Bristol, transferred his activities to Southampton.

But the name of Erskine never really hit the headlines; he was learning the speedway game like most others, the hard way, and he actually retired once for health reasons.

It is not surprising to find that Mike's pre-war speedway years were intermingled with grass track racing whenever time permitted and as an ace in this sport, he raced with considerable success.

Mike designed the famous Farleigh Castle circuit near Trowbridge in Wiltshire. When it opened in 1938 he was racing one of his own products, a Miller Rudge, and the late Reg Stainer was also a notable competitor on a similar machine.

Mike Erskine would arrive at Farleigh with a large and dirty car which contrasted sharply to the pair of beautifully-prepared machines on tow. His models were the fastest and best of the period and when he felt so inclined he would prove it in no uncertain manner, even against the stiffest opposition. The crowds yelled their heads off.

Colin Mead, a prominent grass tracker of that time, and one who eventually won 462 grass track awards, has this to say: "Mike Erskine was without doubt the best engineer riding at that time."

At Farleigh's final meeting in 1938 he raised the track record to 42.85mph, and Mike, the leg-trailer, really provided the thrills. The following year he captained the Farleigh Castle team against Blackmore Vale, both at home and away.

In 1946, the West Wilts. Club made a new track at Farleigh Castle, not far from the old one. But this one was on the side of a hill and situated as it was in a forty-acre field, it provided a super course. Once again, the roar of open exhausts echoed in the valley below where the quiet waters of the Frome meandered along. The old double bridge over the river with the castle ruins perched high above, provided a finishing touch to a unique and, indeed, a picturesque setting.

Post-war Farleigh, until its end in 1954, saw little of Mike Erskine, and I remember him riding there only once. The recognised stars were: Roger Wise, Dick Bradley, Billy Hole, Eric Salmon, Stan Lanfear, Bob Jones, Reg Lambourne and Frank Evans, all of whom took up speedway racing and made names for themselves. But Farleigh had provided the training ground.

On joining Wimbledon however, in 1946, Mike Erskine took speedway racing more seriously, although his progress was still no meteoric rise to the top, but more of a steady methodical ascent. In spite of a broken collar-bone and the fact that he was induced to change his style to foot-forward, which proved quite a tough proposition, he was one of the Don's best scorers, with 82 points in 16 matches.

Then, at the end of the season a team of riders raced at a number of meetings in Germany, at Hanover and Hamburg; Mike was one, and out of five Championship meetings his best performance was third place in the Hanover Individual Championship.

The year 1947 saw Erskine developing into a first-class team man: with his classical track-craft he played a major role in Wimbledon's successful run, in heading the National League table for practically the whole of the season, until the pressure of Wembley and Belle Vue pushed the team into third spot. But, earlier in the season, at New Cross, Mike roared home first in a Final heat to gain him team an exciting League victory over the Wembley champions.

Now comes the Erskine Staride. Mike had come to the conclusion that no matter how good a rider was, if he had not the right kind of frame it was a hundred-to-one chance against him succeeding. And so, throughout the winter of 1947, at his Southampton workshops, he experimented with frames of all shapes and sizes. He found there could not really be a standard frame, as practically every rider required something different. Height, weight and style all entered into the subject. A rider who treated his machine roughly required a stouter gauge of tubing than one who rode his machine moderately. A light frame for the amazing leg-trailer, Oliver Hart, would, of course, be of no use.

Mike took mental notes of the various types of frames that were used by all the top riders, and combining them, he built a jig which, in his opinion, incorporated all the best points of existing frames and his new frame could be made in large quantities.

Eventually the production of the Staride began. This was a complete speedway machine with a JAP engine and its neat insignia on both sides of the tank and the rear mudguard: a circled star with Staride across its middle. The new Erskine job was the talk in the pits all over the country, and Mike was inundated with orders from novices to stars.

As soon as Bill Gilbert rode a Staride in 1948 he shot to the fore and increased his prize money eight-fold. Practically the whole of the Southampton team bought them and Billy Hole and Eric Salmon, who greatly contributed to Bristol's victory in Division Two, were mounted on Erskine Specials.

One of the highlights of the season was the riding of the New Cross skipper, Ron Johnson. He had three

Rider and tuner. That was
Mike Erskine who rode for the
New Cross, Bristol and
Wimbledon teams

The late Alfred Cole, chief
mechanic to the New Cross
team

Starides, each one to suit his style at different circuits and there were five models at New Cross. In League racing
Ron scored 86 per-cent and was runner-up in the British Riders' Championship.

From North to South: from East to West, the orders came rolling in at Erskine's Southampton depot for
the new Staride. From the Beaumont Brothers, Jim Boyd, Tommy Allott, Cliff Watson, Tommy Bateman, Alec
Statham, Norman Parker and Ron Mason, to name but a few.

Graham Warren shot from Third Division status to a test star in a matter of months and he did it on a
Staride. His team-mates too, the late Stan Dell and Doug McLachlan, rode similar models.

Jack Parker first raced one at the 1949 opening New Cross meeting and won the Trinder Trophy: Tommy
Price was riding below par at the start of the 1948 season and, switching to a Staride, wiped up a Newcastle
meeting and later won the World Championship Final in 1949. At the end of this year however, Mike Erskine had
produced about two hundred frames and models and had enough on order to keep him and his staff of seven busy
throughout the winter. He said: "I do not claim that the Staride is the best speedway machine, but it is so easy
to ride that if a fellow cannot ride it, he will never be able to ride any machine."

Freddy Williams took two Starides to Australia for that country's racing season and then became World Champion on one in 1950. Norman Parker took one to New Zealand and other members of the Erskine Brigade included: Bill Pitcher, Norman Price, Ted Bravery, Bert Spencer, Eddie Rigg, Wally Green, Paddy Mills, Geoff Bennett and Bob Fletcher.

These are just a few of the lads who moved faster, and collected more money, thanks to the patience and skill of Mike Erskine. Although his workshops were, of course, a hive of industry, Mike still rode for the "Dons" and he also found time to take over Jack Parker's position as Chairman of the Speedway Riders' Association while Jack was racing in Australia.

Norman Parker, the Wimbledon skipper, was responsible in no small measure for Erskine's racing improvement during 1948 and Mike partnered him in many fine races.

The Staride manufacturer had a good season with the Dons in 1950 and became a World Finalist, but the following one proved unlucky. After a nasty appendix operation early in the year Mike resumed racing. Then came an unfortunate crash at New Cross in July in which he suffered a very painful and unusual injury — a fractured cheek-bone.

Before the 1952 season had begun, Mike Erskine had finally decided to call it a day and retired from active racing. Twenty years in the sport wasn't a bad record. In the meantime however, he had been constructing 500cc racing cars.

The Blackmore Vale Club's grass track meeting at Wiltshire's Willoughby Hedge, near Mere, on April 16, 1961, saw the appearance of a newcomer, and Mike's nineteen year old son Jon was competing in his first-ever meeting. He gained third spot in his heat and final on a 250cc Rudge, which constituted an exceptionally fine first-effort performance.

By the following year, junior Erskine was a true grass track star, now raised into the experts category. 1962 was Jon's initial speedway season and unlike his father, he reached the top within a very short time. Riding for the newly-formed Neath team in Wales he was a heat-leader in a matter of weeks, but, after making three superb performances in the qualifying rounds of the Provincial Riders' Championship, fate stepped in with an injury and kept him out of the Final.

Towards the end of the season, young Jon featured in one of speedway's most spectacular crashes: it was at Leicester that he was catapulted clean over the safety-fence.

Father Mike gave his son a new frame for his twenty-first birthday in February, 1963. Meanwhile Neath had folded up, so Jon signed for Long Eaton. On his way to race at the Nottingham circuit, he often gave me a lunch-time call and, needless to say, his trailer carried two Staride machines. "It's a tough life but a good one," remarked Jon. "I covered over 92,000 miles last year in fulfilling my speedway engagements which, of course, was intersected with grass track racing, but my greatest ambition is to be a farmer!"

Two broken collar-bones collected in grass track spills in 1963 failed to dampen the enthusiasm of this lanky but likeable lad. Other injuries too played havoc with a brilliant career.

Preferring the smoother speedway circuits to the rougher grass tracks, they now claimed him exclusively and speedway's gain was grass track's loss. Joining the Newport team in its initial year, Jon Erskine became one of the heroes in the Wasps success story of 1964 and wedding bells rung for him in the early part of the following year.

NEW CROSS, track of sensational and sentimental memories, and the home of ace mechanic and tuner, ALFRED COLE, from its inception at the start of the 1934 speedway season until its initial closure in 1953. The small South-East London circuit was unfortunately an ill-fated track, for several unsuccessful but gallant attempts have since been made to re-establish the sport in that area.

Alf Cole was one of speedway racing's mechanical minds. Just an ordinary garage mechanic at one time, he rose, in his field of work, to the highest of heights and became Chief Mechanic to the illustrious New Cross team.

But to start at the beginning of his distinguished and superb career, I shall have to take you back to the old Crystal Palace speedway days, and what wonderful days they were. It was in 1931, after the track had been operating for just over three seasons, that Alf Cole looked in one Saturday to see what this dirt track business was all about. His interest in engines naturally led him to the vicinity of the pits and, while watching the various riders, he noticed a youngster who was experiencing trouble.

In offering his assistance the magic touch of Alf Cole initially introduced itself to speedway. That young boy was, of course, Tom Farndon, who was destined to become one of the greatest of all riders.

At the start of the 1934 season, the complete Crystal Palace team, consisting chiefly of Ron Johnson, Harry Shepherd, George Newton, Joe Francis, Tom Farndon and Nobby Key, moved to New Cross speedway, a brand new track of 262 yards and the smallest in Britain. Alf Cole became Farndon's personal tuner and mechanic; it was a great partnership that is certainly part of speedway's exciting history. Both were tremendous friends and they raced greyhounds together.

In that first season the New Cross team won the London Cup and gained third spot in the National League. Three years later the team emulated these achievements and added National League honours to its collection.

By winning the London Riders' Championship in May, 1934, Tom Farndon began a fantastic run of successes which lasted two complete seasons. He broke the New Cross record in the second England v. Australia Test Match; then the Plymouth record fell to him and in the same month (July), as partner to Ron Johnson, won the Best Pairs Trophy at Harringay.

Tom was then nominated to challenge that illustrious Australian, Vic Huxley, and with two magnificent rides, firstly at Wimbledon and then at New Cross, he won the coveted British Individual title, breaking both track records in each case. Farndon now held the three big titles: The National Speedway Champion; the London Champion; and the British Individual Champion — a feat never accomplished by any other rider.

Tom won the Cearns Gold Trophy after beating the late "Bluey" Wilkinson in a decider. Then came elected challenges for the British Individual Championship from team-mate Ron Johnson and Max Grosskreutz. Farndon proved his immense capabilities by retaining the title. His numerous successes still continued throughout 1935, his brilliant leg-trailing style producing a combination of skill, judgement and daring.

Although Tom Farndon had amazing talent he was the first to admit that he owed a great deal to Alf Cole, by his magnificent list of achievements. But sadly, fate decreed that the mighty partnership be broken up. The blackest evening in the history of New Cross speedway occurred on August 28, 1935. It was the last race of the evening (an unimportant scratch one), when Ron Johnson, who was in the lead, touched the fence and fell; Tom was so close behind he could not avoid hitting Ron's machine and was catapulted over the handlebars to land on his head. He died later in hospital from brain injuries.

Alf Cole had lost his bosom friend in a most tragic way. Broken-hearted, he gamely carried on and made arrangements for Mrs Farndon to be represented at the inquest. It was Alf who gave the instructions for the winding-up of Tom's estate; he was one of the bondsmen who guaranteed the due administration; saw to the sale of Tom's greyhounds and, finally, saved Mrs Farndon an estate agent's fee by finding a purchaser for her late husband's house.

"King" Cole really loved his work and his unquenchable thirst was always for further knowledge of riders, frames and motors. He considered, in 1938, that the American, Jack Milne, was the mechanic's ideal rider, and not because he had won the previous year's World Championship. Naturally that reflected great credit on the man who tuned his machines and Jack, as many will remember, was so outstandingly and consistently successful. But these were the least causes of Alf's satisfaction. He regularly dismantled, as a precautionary measure, Jack's motor, but in nine cases out of ten there wasn't a spot or blemish to be found. For that, thanks were due to the American's riding methods.

But there was something more than just mechanical skill behind Alf Cole's superb talent. Much of his success was due to his psychological approach to speedway's many problems in the pits; he placed a lot of faith in friendly chats with the riders which stimulated their riding ability and caused their confidence to improve week by week.

After Tom Farndon's death in 1935, Alf Cole's next protege at New Cross was George Newton, whom he "nursed" to stardom in the same manner. George however, became one of the most discussed riders in the sport with his super-spectacular leg-trailing broadsiding methods, often referred to as quite reckless. Alf, who planned George's races, decided upon his tactics and never hesitated to criticise the young daredevil when he made a mistake.

But the value of Alf Cole could not be measured solely in terms of helpful advice. He provided George with a machine as good as the best of any of his rivals, and one that kept going race after race, without missing a beat. George Newton's frame, shorter and lower than the average, was of no freak design, for he himself was such a diminutive fellow. In only one particular way did his frame depart from the standard practice — the wheelbase was adjustable.

Although George took many chances, he possessed that uncanny sense of balance which characterised the riding of some of speedway's greatest riders. By 1936 he held several New Cross records. He was the real hero of the first England v. Australia Test Match of that year, scoring 16 out of a possible 18 points, and he again rode for his country in the second, fourth and fifth Tests. Reaching the World Final in the following season and breaking no less than three records at New Cross, made him a real idol of the "Old Kent Road" enthusiasts.

On March 30, (1938) George gained the most coveted and the remaining 4-lap, clutch-start record on his home circuit. And throughout the season the Newton Wonder, still in the orange and black race colours, provided his usual abundance of thrills. It was his finest year, and in the fifth Test Match at Wimbledon he captained the English side which made it his seventh Test appearance.

Mechanical breakdowns in the early days of speedway racing, detracted from the sport as a spectacle, but this was reduced to very small dimensions when a few track managements commenced to maintain their own teams' machines in communal workshops. The Crystal Palace promoters were the pioneers of the movement in 1931, and since moving to New Cross the same management was well to the forefront in the matter of equipment. Details of maintenance costs of this particular track may be interesting and perhaps astonishing too. I take 1935 as a typical pre-war year.

At New Cross, the total cost of maintenance was about £2,500, and remember this was over forty years ago. It covered ten machines and included the wages paid to five qualified mechanics, the head of whom was Alfred Cole. The cost included rent for the premises, fuel, spares purchased during the season and renewals. Messrs. Mockford and Smith were careful not to "spoil their ship for a ha'porth of tar," but on the other hand were quite satisfied that not a penny was being wasted.

Wages were a big item: over £800 for the season, which presented a great contrast to the immediate post-war years, in which a good mechanic alone would draw approximately that figure.

Still bigger, were the accounts for spares and with regard to renewals, 53 pistons and 21 new cylinder barrels were purchased. Piston rings were renewed in the team's motors for every match; 470 of them were used, together with 282 sets of valve springs. Five front tyres had to be bought and 55 rear ones! Other purchases included 33 steering damper friction discs; 35 feet of rubber tubing for the flexible petrol pipes and 16 carburettor floats. Chains, too, were a heavy item, 17 primary and 28 rear ones, which, in view of the tremendous strain imposed upon them, was considered quite reasonable by Alf Cole.

In spite of the number of crashes, only 15 new wheels were acquired, and likewise, only 16 new racing plugs were needed throughout the season. The track maintenance of machines was an expensive business, but it certainly paid good dividends to the promoters.

As the years went by, Alf Cole remained faithful to the work to which he was so deeply dedicated. He began to work wonders with the young Australian, the late Ray Duggan (Vic's brother) but the war intervened in September, 1939, and racing was brought to an inevitable and sudden halt. The very sad loss of his brother, Ray, who was killed in January, 1950, in a triple crash at Sydney speedway (Australia) when Norman Clay was also killed in the same pile-up, speeded Vic Duggan's own retirement from the sport.

During World War Two, Alf Cole served, and not without distinction, in the London Fire Force Dispatch Riders' Organisation as a Divisional Officer. He had complete charge of all its motorcycles.

So appreciative was the body of his unceasing efforts to train and maintain its force, for which Alf was chiefly responsible, that the organisation made him a presentation of an illuminated address and a gold watch. That was in 1944.

With the war over, speedway racing was soon resumed and, not surprisingly, Alf Cole returned to the New Cross workshops, still under the management of his old and valued friends, Fred Mockford and Cecil Smith.

The officials and enthusiasts alike, attending the "Rangers" meeting on April 17, 1946, officially opened by the Mayor of Deptford, were impressed with the excellent condition of the team's machines. When racing ceased at the end of the 1939 season, the New Cross machines, eight in number, were most carefully overhauled, well greased, and stored.

Then Alf Cole had turned his attention to the large stock of spares. All these were wrapped up and buried well away from the threats of enemy action, and many well remember how often the New Cross area was hit by bombs.

On being resurrected, these spares, invaluable at that particular time because of an acute shortage, were found in perfect condition.

At the start of the 1946 season, Star-maker Cole spotted that there were possibilities in the pre-war Wimbledon reserve, Eric French, the 30 year old Tadworth carpenter. So Alf took him in hand with the result that Eric immediately jumped to the front. In two weeks his time for the four laps dropped by four seconds: he gave a dashing display in the opening New Cross matches which gained him a permanent place in the team. Alf had previously predicted a great future for Eric French and how right he was, as Eric remained a Ranger for many years, securing runner-up position in the '49 London Riders' Championship. He went on to captain the team in 1952 and until New Cross initially, closed in the middle of 1953. It is sad to relate that the English test star, the much beloved Eric, died in February, 1974.

Mechanics and riders regarded machines as almost human. Moreover Alf Cole thought that it was indeed a poor machine that did not possess a personality peculiarly its own. Take for example, a frame that was constructed for Ron Johnson. He soon found this particular model was going to take some riding, and try as he did, the tiger he could not tame. It threw him; rode over him and pushed him into safety fences! Alf Cole appropriately christened it "The Killer," a breaker of hearts and limbs, and for sixteen years it remained the terror of the tracks.

Like the promoters Fred Mockford and Cecil Smith, and rider Ron Johnson, Alf was part of the Crystal Palace/New Cross tradition, and acknowledged as one of the greatest maintenance men the sport has ever known. A host of riders owed much of their success to his mechanical and tuning ability. Jack Milne, Stan Greatrex, Bill Longley, Ron Johnson and Cyril Roger, to name but a few, and each and every one benefitted by his skill and kindly advice.

The rider, of course, gives you the spectacular side of speedway racing, but the mechanics and tuners are the king-pins around which the sport revolves. Unseen by the general public and definitely unsung, they work feverishly at the tuning bench or in the heart of the pits, their expert hands making quick adjustments at amazing speed, perhaps bringing a life-time of technical knowledge to bear upon a troublesome motor. The fate of a star rider, or even the fortunes of a whole team, depends upon their skill.

When Bert Roger was recalled from Exeter to join his brother Cyril at New Cross he soon developed into a top-grade rider. He remarked: "I owe no end of gratitude to Alf Cole as he did a great deal in getting me to the forefront."

In a short speech, made after his World Championship win in 1953, Freddie Williams paid tribute to the work of his mechanic. It was nice to see that occasionally "the back room boys" were given a little of the limelight, for enthusiasts did not and do not, always realise that it takes more than the riders themselves to make the wheels go round.

Mechanics and tuners are all part and parcel of speedway racing; they get little praise, yet, if it wasn't for them, racing would be in a complete turmoil. They have always been, and still are, as vital to the sport as the riders themselves, and at times their work can be equally exacting.

You have been reading a little of three of speedway's greatest "back room boys." There are others, of course, but Alf Cole, in acknowledging his various arts of Chief Mechanic, Tuner, Star-maker, Team-Manager, his successes, and his length of speedway service, is probably the most illustrious.

As October, 1964 came round, Alf Cole had tuned his last motor. On the thirteenth of that month he was conveyed to New Cross hospital suffering from cancer. To the dismay of his countless friends and admirers he died (aged 60) on August 7, of the following year, leaving his wife, to whom he had been married for thirty seven years, and one son who was then in the Fleet Air Arm.

The loss of ALF COLE was a great blow to many, and none-the-less to speedway racing in general. He left a gap in the lives of his intimate friends, and a bigger one in that of his wife Kitty, a gap which unfortunately, can never be filled.

An immensely likeable fellow, he was more than a famous mechanic, tuner and adviser, which can be regarded as almost secondary considerations. He was a genuine friend, guide and philosopher to a host of riders and people, and certainly one of the best we shall ever have. Whatever the circumstances, Alf was ever constant, always cheerful, quiet, modest, kind and considerate — superb virtues that are hard to equal, let alone surpass.

SPEEDWAY RACING is richer for having ALF COLE'S distinguished company ... it is greatly the poorer for his passing.

12 They pay to serve

Continually, year in and year out, hundreds of speedway and grass track meetings take place throughout the season, up and down the country. They are attended by the St.John Ambulance Brigade and far too little praise is given to their invaluable work. Members give of their best and their presence and skill give the riders additional confidence.

British membership of the Brigade totals well over 300,000 and its origin can be traced back many hundreds of years. Besides having a renowned history, the Brigade has also an equally interesting one. Few public gatherings are complete without the familiar sight of their black and white uniforms.

The origin of the Order of the Hospital of St.John of Jerusalem, generally known in the Middle Ages simply as the Knights Hospitallers, is so ancient that its foundation has been ascribed to Judas Maccebaeus. Its real origin is to be found in the hospice for pilgrims, established in Jerusalem in A.D.600 by Abbot Probus. The Order still maintains the Hospital of St.John of Jerusalem, where today opthalmic treatment is provided without distinction of race, class or creed.

In England, around 1144, the Hospitallers built their Priory at Clerkenwell in London. The Order suffered a fierce persecution under King Henry VIII, and its estates were confiscated by Queen Elizabeth in 1559. But a series of Grand Priors of England continued to be appointed by the Knights of Malta until 1831, when the Order was re-established in England.

1873 however, saw the Order secure possession of St.John's Gate, the remains of the ancient Priory of Clerkenwell, and there today the present Chancery of the Order is housed.

The Saint John Ambulance Brigade was established in 1887 and consists of a body of qualified uniformed members, whose efficiency is maintained by constant practice and annual re-examination. It exists in order to render First Aid to the sick and injured on public occasions and each year Brigade members deal with more than half-a-million cases.

In May, 1956, twenty thousand members from home and overseas were reviewed in London's Hyde Park by Her Majesty Queen Elizabeth, the Sovereign Head of the Order; Brigade members give around four million hours' voluntary service every year!

Previously, in 1954, the Brigade celebrated a continuous history of sixty years of activity in Wembley, the Divisions of which were founded in 1893 by Dr.C.E.Goddard, after an accident at Wembley railway station.

Today, St.John is welcomed by the public, but it is interesting to recall that the conditions under which the Brigade carried out its duties in the early days were the reverse of encouraging, and one cannot but admire the tremendous courage of the early pioneers. A section of the medical profession were openly hostile to the movement; the public were indifferent, if not sceptical, and the rabble greeted the appearance of men in the St.John uniform with cries of "body-snatchers".

Their successors certainly owe to them a debt which can be repaid only by what they, in turn, pass on to ensuing generations, and help to carry on the tradition of the Order of St.John, the oldest Order of Chivalry in existence.

As part of their public duty, members annually give thousands of hours to voluntary attendances, and motorcycle race meetings form only a part of their comprehensive service. At cinemas; ceremonial parades; at seaside resorts and all kinds of places where crowds congregate, the Brigade is always there — watching and caring.

The work of the Brigade is entirely voluntary and no aid of any sort is given by the State.

Without thought for themselves, at their own cost and sacrifice, they hold true to their double motto:
"FOR THE FAITH: FOR THE SERVICE OF MANKIND."

13 The speedway collectors

Time certainly marches on ... and as the years go hurriedly by and dirt track machines that were manufactured in the late 1920s and early 1930s become more scarce, more legendary and more valuable, they therefore become more and more sought after by Vintage enthusiasts. Today, these very early models of which, regretfully, only a few now remain, have a beauty all their own, a romance in their own right. And rightly so.

For a great number of fans, the story of the men who designed, built and tuned these machines for a specialised sport, has a romantic fascination as well as an admiration for those intrepid riders who so gallantly rode them leg-trailing style.

Here then, are a few of today's speedway collectors.

BOB JONES, the Swindonian, is a life-long addict of motorcycle racing. In fact, like Bill Davies, one can justifiably describe him as a super-enthusiast. A notable speedway and grass track rider during the late 'forties and 'fifties, his exploits can be traced back to the mid 'thirties. Today he rides only in an occasional Vintage event.

In Bob's collection, besides a dirt track Rudge, is a Douglas Red Devil, originally purchased from Claude Rye, a former Wimbledon skipper. It was in 1930 that this particular machine made its appearance and only a small number were made. They differed from the Douglas Company's other speedway models in several ways. For instance a different cam was employed; they were the firm's only models running purely on dope and they had a narrower tank, nickel-plated, with a red transfer of a different shape. Specially tuned by Bert Dixon, these unique machines had a 9 to 1 compression ratio and were clutchless. RD1 was their fuel and, enamelled all red, they had a quickly detachable cinder-guard. On the frame's head a brilliant transfer took the form of a Scotsman holding high in the air a 350 engine with one hand! Which all went to demonstrate the lightness of the Douglas motor.

The Red Devils however, were the last of the long-stroke Douglas dirt track machines and although some of the machine's history seems rather obscure, it appears certain that these models did exist. They were a by-product of tuner Bert Dixon, more closely associated with Wimbledon speedway in the post-war era.

It was in a Vintage event at Coventry speedway when Bob Jones, on the Red Devil was beaten on the straights by the old-time notability, "Squib" Burton, who shot up the straights like a rocket. Bob knew full well he had one of the fastest Duggies in the country, of 494cc of course, and only fathomed out the mystery the next time he met "Squib", the Leicester Team Manager. Apparently there were two Devils in that particular race, for Cyril Burton confessed that he was riding one of the old 600cc Duggies! "The Old Devil," remarked Bob in his characteristically laughing manner.

A jolly good rider; a good fellow in every sense of the word; a thorough sportsman and above all, there's that ever-helpful hand, as always, extended to the star and novice alike. This typifies the popular Swindonian, and what better characteristic traits can anyone have than these?

The history of Blunsdon speedway certainly draws attention to the evergreen Bob Jones, who this year begins his 28th consecutive season with Swindon.

Rider; Captain of the team; Track Record Holder; Team Manager and Chief Mechanic, "Joner" has really been through the lot at Blunsdon. All the old originals have long since disappeared from the scene, but Bob still remains, not only as a faithful allegiance holder to Swindon speedway, but as a brilliant example of motorcycle enthusiasm of the first magnitude.

A lifetime totally dedicated to the motorcycle sport. That is the super record of Kenneth Robert Jones. One cannot do better than that.

Talking over old times; Bob Jones (right) with Bill Davies (centre) and the author. Bob's original Douglas "Red Devil" purchased from Claude Rye is in front

Below, 56-year-old Bill Davies tries his 1929 dirt track "Duggie" at Hackney Speedway in 1970, in preparation for the evening's 'old-time' event

The 1928 Motorcycle Show was memorable for an aspect that was entirely new to the motorcycle scene, for the dirt track models were making their debut. Almost every major manufacturer had a speedway machine on display. Some, like the Rudge Whitworth, a particularly dazzling model, and the Douglas, were the genuine article.

For patience and meticulous restoration one has to hand it to Dave McMahon, a 40 year old motor mechanic from Coventry, for it has taken him ten years to complete his labour of love project, that of building an original 1928 dirt track Rudge.

Beginning with just the engine, which bears DT markings, on its special crankcase, Dave completed his 10 year quest for the remaining parts through swapping, advertising, and the tracking down of grapevine rumours. Its design includes many features which were probably advanced for its year. As it was designed specifically for speedway racing, it has no footrest for the rider's left foot, but there is a right-hand footrest and a sizeable knee hook.

Beautifully made is the polished brass wedge-shaped fuel tank with the Rudge Whitworth circular stop hand insignia on either side. Says Dave: "I made four tanks before I was completely satisfied."

There is a rigid centre-stand, quite authentic, and the "gearbox" is a Rudge single-speed countershaft and clutch unit. What immediately strikes one is the vast area of chromium-plating; the front forks, the mudguards, the exhaust pipes and the frame struts. The Rudge Company had their shiny parts plated by a specialist cutlery firm in Sheffield!

Initially in dirt track racing no one really had a clue of what kind of machine was the ideal model, hence the outrigger tubes to give absolute rigidity. Many other works models employed the use of these extra frame struts, and only at a later date was it found that a degree of frame whip was, in fact, an advantage.

Dave McMahon has ridden the model in exhibition runs at Wolverhampton and Coventry tracks and he even took it to Malory Park for three seasons on the trot 1969-71, for the Vintage Race of the Year parades.

Today, the dirt track Rudge Whitworth can be seen in all its immaculate glory at Stanford Hall, near Rugby. It's a delight to all who view it.

Vintage enthusiast Dave McMahon of Coventry displays his magnificent 1928 works dirt track Rudge-Whitworth

Len Cole's unique trio of 1928-1929 dirt track Douglases

Billy Dallison sitting astride the dirt track Douglas with Jack Parker and the works Douglas tuner, the late Freddie Dixon (right), outside the factory

BILL DAVIES, the chubby-faced happy-go-lucky veteran, covers fantastically high mileages in search for his obvious enjoyment — that of competing in Vintage events, in fact he is acknowledged as the King of the Vintagers whether in speedway or on the grass. He's one of these rare super-enthusiasts and owns and races a pukka dirt track 1929 Douglas ... he's a sportsman of the highest order.

A cool, tough, dedicated and an immensely likeable and even-tempered fellow, and as one rider puts it; "You'll never find him in a flap; he's certainly a great asset to the racing game."

To racing enthusiasts it is evident that Bill still lives for the sport, even though his days of riding modern grass track machinery are practically over. He initially took up grass track racing in 1933 and his first-ever success was on a dirt track Douglas which can be seen today in Murray's Museum in the Isle of Man.

Besides the Duggie, Bill owns a further thirty models, in his amazing Vintage, post-Vintage and Veteran collection, which could probably be claimed as the largest specialist private owner collection in the country, if not in the world. Speedwaywise, his machines include: two 1929 Douglases, a 1930 Rudge JAP, a 1931 Rudge, a 1939 Martin JAP, a "Chipchase" JAP and a 1946 Brine JAP.

The annals of grass track racing certainly draw attention to a long service medal, earned by one of our more durable pillars of the sport. That's, of course, Bill Davies who probably holds the longevity record. Forty three years in the sport is a very long time!

On the Rudge JAP, Bill won the Vintage Trophy at Weymouth speedway's Wessex Championships in 1973 and repeated the achievement the following year. Runner-up in the National Open Vintage Championship in 1971 and '72, he later won the event outright. Winning the Vintage Wessex Championship was another link in a chain of victories. And it is often said that it's the tough times that inspire man to exercise his genius to the full. There's certainly a lot of truth in this. At least it inspired Bill to keep ahead of his greatest rival, Adrian Kessell, in this important meeting and he gained the Vintage Championship Trophy. His average speed was so fast on the 1930 Rudge JAP that he was able to line up in the Open Fastest Twelve Riders' event! What a rider!

As you have guessed this Vintage notability lives life to the full. Speedway or grass; sand or shale; it makes no difference to versatile Bill Davies. He simply loves it all and what is more, blessed as he is with the great virtue of an even-temper, makes his racing ... all that more enjoyable.

LEONARD COLE, is certainly a modest man and to get him to talk about himself is well-nigh impossible. But the fact remains that as a tuner he is one of the country's leading authorities on racing Douglases; he's also a luminary of the National Sprint Association.

It was not so long ago that Len owned three 1929 dirt track Douglases, the marque which still provokes looks of admiration whenever seen, which was probably the largest collection of this make in the world. But one has now been sold to an American enthusiast.

As a schoolboy, Len paid his admission fee of sixpence (2½p) in 1928, to watch the Crystal Palace Path Race meetings on a Saturday afternoon, when Gus Kuhn (Calthorpe) was usually one of the stars. He would then see the nearby dirt track meetings in the evenings, and then, after that, he used to enter the giant Crystal Palace itself to listen to the massive organ, and all for the same sixpence!

The enthusiastic 14 year old youngster hung around the speedway pits, like all schoolboys do, and often helped to unload the dirt machines from the lorry of a visiting team. His heroes at that time included Charlie Datson and Paddy Dean, the two renowned Douglas exponents ... all the way from Australia. And from those very early days he has always been a Duggie fanatic. Not surprisingly too as these particular machines have always carried a great affection for those who rode them and for those who were fortunate enough to watch them in action. Even today, they are a magnet to many.

It was however, in 1955 that Len Cole staged a demonstration with his then 27 year old Douglases. This took place at Wimbledon on a pouring wet autumn day and the rain sodden circuit did not provide the best conditions for the flat twins. Phil Bishop, the chosen rider, made several runs and on one he came a real cropper!

Since then, Len Cole's Duggies, together with those of Bob Jones' and Bill Davies', have been brought out for many exhibition runs at several tracks, thus providing an added attraction to speedway's rather monotonous set-up.

REX JUDD and FREDDIE DIXON were the official Douglas speedway tuners at the Bristol factory from 1928-30. Both had been two of the country's top racing men and both rode Douglas machines with remarkable success. Few men have become legendary figures during their lifetime, but Fred was one. To have known him as many did, was to have caught a glimpse of those rugged Elizabethan characters whose ceaseless search for

*Bristolians Roy Nowell and
Eric Haskins on their 1929
dirt track Douglases on which
they thrilled the grass track
crowds in the late sixties*

adventure laid the foundations of Britain's greatness. Hundreds of stories have been told of him, few of them apocryphal; indeed, the more improbable the tale, the more likely it was to be true!

Rex Judd, tough and pugnacious, originally joined the illustrious Douglas racing team at Brooklands in 1922 and, in the following year gained the world's flying kilometre record (750cc class) at over 98mph, his fastest speed in one direction being 102.37mph. In accomplishing this notable feat, he became the first rider to exceed the century mark in that class.

Once started, Rex's career as a professional rider assumed a spectacular, steep trajectory. He possessed, both physically and mentally, just the right attributes that the game demanded. Slightly built and short in stature, he had a valuable knack of packing himself into a tight, wind-cheating ball, and it paid great dividends, particularly on the vast Brooklands course.

During 1923 he won every scratch race at Brooklands in which he competed, and two years later won the Nisbet Award in the Senior TT. But to record even the bare bones of his track racing exploits over five competitive years with Douglases would probably fill a volume!

Rex and Freddie both left the Douglas firm during 1930, each to make his mark in totally different spheres. Fred took up car racing, and Rex turned his attention to the commercial side of the movement and established a motorcycle business in North West London.

Later, he became a collector and secured one of the finest individual collections of Vintage machines in the world. And one of the largest too, which included what is reputed to be the oldest motorcycle in the world — an 1898 4-cylinder Holden, the complete model being made in Kennington.

On occasions there are various groups of motorcycle enthusiasts intently looking in the large window of 415 Burnt Oak Broadway, Edgware. And it's not surprising for at times on display is a beautifully-kept 1928 dirt track Douglas. The fine exhibit is, of course, one of the late Rex Judd's, now handed down to his son Peter, who still continues the motorcycle business that his father originally founded in 1931.

ROY NOWELL and ERIC HASKINS of the Bristol Club were racing dirt track Douglases on the grass in the late 'sixties, and what is more they were both leg-trailers! At that particular time, Vintage events were becoming increasingly popular and, of course, they still are. Eric formed his own contingent of Vintage boys. His and Roy's full-blooded spectacular riding delighted the crowds and their style sounded a chord in many hearts, bringing back great memories of the olden days.

Believed to be the only one now in existence, here is Jeff Clew's 1929 dirt track Velocette

Both the Bristolians were a super attraction on various circuits for quite a number of seasons, and Eric won the Founders Trophy of the Southern Centre Riders' Association. He was a fine personality, full of infectious good humour and a sparkling Vintage exponent.

You might ask. "How did the times of these Vintagers compare with the modern JAP's?" It sounds incredible, but over an ordinary 4-lap race there was only a few seconds in it, and yet a difference of nearly forty years in the ages of the machines! Their price in 1929? £85. Their price today? who knows?

Eric Haskins eventually sold his "Duggie" to Bill Davies who, at 56 still races it, and successfully too. The combined ages of Bill and his machine total over one hundred years!

Roy Nowell's father died in 1968 and Roy's interest in the sport unfortunately died too. Although he hasn't ridden his model for a considerable period, he still owns it ... just one of the few remaining models that were all the rage in speedway racing 47 years ago!

14 Speedway mascots of the early days

TEAM MASCOTS, a tradition in speedway's early years, are very much less in evidence today. The Crystal Palace team once had a lion cub and Triss Sharp made a great friend of it. Southampton had "Tink" Bryant, but previously it had a fox cub which had a particular liking for George Bishop's helmet! Bristol, had a handsome bulldog ... Wembley had two lions that couldn't be tamed and, of course, up and down the country there were many other mascots.

But speedway's first-ever Team Mascot was Ian Hoskins, who used to lead the notable Wembley "Lions" around the track. He made his debut on Whit Monday, 1930, when he headed the Grand Parade on his specially-built miniature motorcycle, capable of a speed of 30mph. Ian however, was actually preceded by Walter Brierley (not a mascot) who came from Edinburgh, and as early as 1929, the seven year old wonder motorist and broadsider gave an exhibition in a Baby Austin Seven and afterwards established a solo 2-lap track figure.

By 1930, young Walter held the Juvenile track record at Wembley by clocking 101.4 seconds. This was a two-lap rolling start affair. Despite the fact of the Senior 4-lap record at 79.4 seconds, then held by Colin Watson, Walter's time was indeed a creditable one. Now came an official attack on his record on June 12, (1930), by Ian Hoskins with his Fruin Special. And he failed! 143 seconds was not good enough, but he made another attempt. His time: 108.4 seconds.

However, at Wembley's final meeting of the season, six year old Ian attacked that elusive record once again and, for him, it was third time lucky. He carved nearly fifteen seconds off Walter Brierley's time in turning a time of 86.8 seconds. Incidentally, at that particular time, the Empire Stadium track was composed of a surface of cinders two feet in depth! Rough cinders at the bottom and very fine on the top.

Ian Hoskins spent his first birthday (in 1925) at Maitland, in Australia, howling to the beat of the band, because he couldn't go to the newly-opened speedway! His second birthday was spent at the speedway Royale, Sydney, and his third spent smiling at the blacks along the track of the railway line over the vast Nullabor Plains on his two thousand mile railway trip from Sydney to Western Australia. Here he saw Stan Catlett, Syd Parsons, Ron Johnson, Alf Chick and lots of other boys who were learning to master the art of speedway riding.

Ian's fourth birthday found him on board a ship coming through the Suez Canal on his way to merry England and his fifth was spent in good old Wembley. For a birthday present Harry Whitfield, a Wembley team rider, gave him a coloured crash helmet and for his sixth birthday, which he spent just after returning from Spain, where he watched the Spaniards learning to race, young Ian was given a miniature motorcycle.

After three seasons managing the Wembley Lions his father, Johnnie, moved to West Ham in 1932 and Ian still circled the Hammer's track, but he was now riding another machine, an Excelsior-JAP, one of the most beautiful miniature models ever seen. His younger brother Jack had one too.

In the late 'forties, under the tuition of his father, Ian Hoskins, at the age of 25, became speedway's youngest-ever promoter, and he managed Glasgow's White City track with great success. He was boss of the famous Edinburgh Monarchs for no less than eight years, and in those eight seasons, the gay cavalier of Scottish speedway, had used a galaxy of riders in his team; some from Norway, Sweden, Austria, Denmark, Scotland, England, New Zealand and Australia.

Edinburgh speedway certainly leaves behind a proud record of achievement ... and a host of happy memories.

A grand parade at Wembley in 1931. The world's premier speedway rider, Vic Huxley with young Ian Hoskins, the team's mascot, and Colin Watson

Five years later Ian Hoskins was the mascot of the West Ham team. He is seen here on his miniature Martin-JAP

15 Good lookers~ but fierce rivals

It was certainly not an uncommon sight in the 1920's or in the 1930's for that matter, to see a contingent of girl competitors in motorcycling sporting events. They usually met the menfolk on equal terms and at times caused a great sensation in beating them. Take for instance the 1927 International Six Days Trial, the biggest event of the motorcycling calendar, when the English Ladies' team lost a mere five marks and won the International Vase Trophy. What a superb victory! In fact the team actually lost fewer marks than the all-man Trophy team. Marjorie Cottle (348 Douglas), Louie McLean (348 Douglas) and Edyth Foley (494 Triumph) were the girls in question. All three won a Gold Medal in the same event the following year.

Majorie and Edyth plus Eva Askquith and Fay Taylour competed in freak hill climbs such as the famous Post Hill at Leeds, which has a one-in-one gradient. Then there was Dalton Bank at Huddersfield. Meetings at these venues drew crowds from 8 - 15,000 spectators several times a year and the girl riders were tremendous attractions.

While all this was going on, girls like the notable Marjorie Dare were flashing round the Wall-of-Death at terrifying speeds, defying all the laws of gravity as they rode their machines horizontal fashion around the inside of a massive wooden cylinder.

It was not surprising therefore, to see a batch of girls racing on the cinders. This was in 1929. Girls such as "Babs" Nield, Jessie Hole, "Sunny Somerset," Gladys Thornhill, Dot Cowley, Eva Askquith and Fay Taylour, the latter two being far and away the best of this little group and really in a class of their own. They both had the skill, judgement and courage that many experienced males might have envied; they were the real champions of their own fair sex, and their names became household words throughout the country.

Fay Taylour was born at Birr, King's County, Ireland and was educated at Alexandra College, Dublin. By the time her college days were over she claimed a sporty and lively nature, making a host of good friends, but coming to live in an English country town things seemed rather dull and slow in comparison. She thought that something on wheels might brighten her life and so she purchased a tiny two-stroke motorcycle, springing the acquisition upon a startled family.

But it was not long before Miss Taylour desired to be a bigger and better motorcyclist. She bought a 348cc AJS and proceeded to take a bold bite at the competition apple by riding the machine in the Camberley Club's famous Southern Scott scramble on March 5, 1927. This particular event ranked supreme in the minds of rough riders. It was held on Camberley Heath, a circuit of some 24 miles, being covered once in the morning and once in the afternoon.

Heavy rain made the course extremely difficult, but Fay was not alone in her efforts for Marjorie Cottle, Edyth Foley and Louie McLean were the three other girls who battled with the atrocious conditions. Enthusiastic Fay on the AJS proved the best of the bunch and in making top performance by a girl competitor was awarded the Venus Trophy, which initially marked the beginning of her competitive motorcycle career.

Two months later the Camberley Club staged that memorial dirt track meeting over a sandy course on the heath, to which I have already made mention in a previous chapter. It was here that the remarkable Fay Taylour gained great success in beating every male competitor except one! C.Harman had the audacity to put her into second place in the 350cc event but Fay won the Unlimited cc Trophy for gaining first place on her 348cc AJS in that event, beating the boys on bigger machines — W.Shearing (497 Ariel) and G.Beard (493 Sunbeam) into second and third spots respectively.

1929. Fay Taylour (left) *raises her face mask to give the photographer a smile, prior to a Match Race with Eva Askquith at Wembley*

After successes in the National Cotswold and Kickham Cup Trials, Fay took on a secretarial job at Rudge Whitworth Ltd., but more often than not she was found in the competition department and not in the advertisement section, where she belonged.

Purely on merit alone she was elected to ride as a member of the official Rudge trials team, sharing a great responsibility with Jack Amott and Peter Blamire ... her speedway fame was yet to come.

This adventurous girl won the special Ladies' award in the London-to-Gloucester-to-London Trial and on Maidens Grove, the most difficult hill, the Rudge entry was particularly outstanding.

Still with Rudge's in 1928, Miss Taylour was now a prominent figure in the trials world; she revelled in riding against the majority of England's most famous riders, winning Gold Medals in the National Alan and Travers Trophy Trials; Silver Medals in the Colmore (in which there were 218 participants), Cotswold and Victory Trophy Trials; Bronze Medals in the Bemrose Trial and the Wood Green M.C. Ladies' Trial; a first-class award in the Leeds £200 Trial and a Gold Medal in the ACU Six Days Trial, run over a 750 mile route in which Fay only lost three marks!

By now dirt track racing had been established in England and Miss Taylour often watched the racing at Stamford Bridge. Soon she was found to be doing intensive practice at the Crystal Palace track and a little later on, still riding her trials Rudge, she took on Ron Johnson (Harley) in a match race, but unfortunately fell off in both heats, much to the annoyance of Fred Mockford who told her if she kept falling off, girls would be barred from the tracks.

A new machine however, a Rudge Special, brought her better luck and Fay gained considerable success especially in the North. She was popular wherever she raced and at Liverpool received a great ovation for her fearless riding with the pioneer Australian, Keith McKay in a Silver Armlet final.

In a match race at the Crystal Palace with Joe Francis, this 24 year old girl, promptly left him at the start and he fell from his Ariel in trying to catch her! Fay rode at the Brighton and Edinburgh tracks and gained the ladies' record at Brandon. Soon after, she was at the Crystal Palace with a gleaming brand new dirt track Douglas and how that Duggie could move! It astounded everyone.

In November Fay left England to race in Australia, taking her Douglas, the Rudge as a standby, and a spare engine. This courageous girl travelled all alone; she had no racing engagements apart from the one that Johnnie Hoskins had fixed up for her at Perth plus a few introductory letters and recommendations. For a man this would have been a big undertaking: for a woman doubly so.

12,000 miles is a very long journey and Fay didn't land down-under before January, 1929. Australia gave her a grand reception. She liked the big half-mile Perth circuit. "You can enjoy a slide because you can stay in it" she remarked.

After beating Frank Brown in a match race at over 52mph, at Claremont, Miss Taylour took on the renowned Sig Schlam. This particular race resulted in a victory for Fay, who won at 54.9mph, thereby equalling a record which, until Sig had lowered it the previous week, had stood for a year.

This female speedway star drew a record crowd at Brisbane, her fastest lap on the quarter mile track being turned at just over 44mph. After returning to England in April, 1929, Fay Taylour gained the flying-lap record at Wembley at 37mph, and there it remained for quite a while. Then it took no less a famous rider than Max Grosskreutz to relieve her of the honour, but Max clocked only 2/5th of a second less!

Racing again in Australia's ensuing season with other English riders — Roger Frogley, Arthur Atkinson and Jack Ormston, Fay's tour, which this time took in New Zealand, proved immensely successful and she returned with a considerable amount of prize money. She returned also to find that several London promoters had made the decision to ban girl riders from their tracks, but following swiftly on the heels of that decision came the news that newcomer Miss Gladys Thornhill, a sixteen year old, had been granted an ACU licence and had signed on for the Sheffield management. Clem Beckett and "Skid" Skinner were loaning her machines and giving her tuition. So the girl riders were still not officially barred by the sport's governing body.

Miss Taylour seemed generally disappointed with the English speedway set-up and said in one of her interviews: "The boys are just as wonderful as ever they were, but somehow racing has become too much like professional football and I cannot work up any enthusiasm for the League business." She then went to Germany and won a match race at Hamburg speedway against the other girls — "Babs" Neild and Gladys Thornhill.

"Babs" and Gladys were great favourites at the Manchester tracks (Belle Vue and White City), as also was Dot Cowley, daughter of the notable road racer, "Pa" Cowley. Dot was an accomplished motorcyclist who raced a Scott on Southport sands and later in World War Two gave valuable service in the WVS.

In the south there was Miss "Sunny Somerset" who rode under a cinders nom-de-plume, thought up by Johnnie Hoskins which hid the identity of Vera Hole. She was a native of Somerset and although never in the Taylour-Askquith class as a dirt track rider, she certainly knew how to handle her dirt track Douglas of the day. Later she was found to be in a miniature garden business.

In one way Fay Taylour thought she ought to give up dirt track racing and begin being a little more dignified, but she found its fascination too strong. "It's a great game," she said.

EVA ASKQUITH, a tough Yorkshire girl, thought it a great game too. But it was several years before dirt track racing started in this country that Eva became motorcycle minded. Her first ever machine was a 250cc New Imperial; then came a faster model, an HRD and after that a special TT AJS, which she rode in a Scott Trial, acknowledged as the greatest one-day trial in the country. Merely to complete the course was a physical feat of the Herculean type. The very severe nature of it with gullies; torrential streams; rocks; mud; water holes; bogs; bracken; heather and atrocious gradients, always took its toll of the courageous competitors. They all ached from head to foot at the finish and were almost dazed by fatigue. All that really mattered was for the competitors to be able to say that they finished! And that is exactly what Eva Askquith said after the 1927 event, but how many times the "Ajay" threw her off is not really known!

Everyone was full of praise for the tenacity and courage displayed by twentyone year old Eva. She won a second class award. There were other competitors too in that great sporting event who were destined for speedway fame. Oliver Langton and his brother Eric were riding 596cc Scott machines, and Alec Jackson (speedway manager

A superb photograph posed as if "Baby faced" Dot Cowley could and should never be seated on anything other than a dirt track Douglas

at Wembley for many, many years from 1932) rode a 490cc Norton. Oliver won the Bailey Trophy and the Denham Award; Alec gained the special award, while Oliver and Eric, with Tommy Hatch, carried off the Scott Trophy for the best amateur team.

Eva Askquith now purchased a Velocette. Quite a nice machine and one that brought her into the limelight. She used it for grass track racing, for freak hill climbing at Post Hill and at Dalton Bank, and for reliability trials.

A very clever performance of Eva's was at Dalton Bank, when she crossed the finishing line at the top of the freak hill on one wheel in an almost vertical position! A photographer captured this spectacular feat, and his picture appeared in the next day's newspapers with a caption — "Girl rider's spectacular feat."

Recording the fastest time at a Post Hill event in the ladies' class against Marjorie Cottle (Raleigh), Edyth Foley (Triumph) and Fay Taylour (Ariel), Eva was awarded the Ladies Trophy — a most attractive Cup. Two years later Eva and Fay were fighting it out on the dirt tracks instead of up an almost perpendicular hill!

Miss Askquith also took part in sand meetings but she never really liked this sprint-type event. It was the "flat-out" freak hill climbs that she really enjoyed, although grass track racing on the Harrogate cricket ground provided her with an immense amount of fun, and successes too.

Jack Barnett and Eva Askquith (12) both on dirt track Douglases, shake hands before their special Match Race at King's Oak in 1929

In 1928, just as the majority of dirt tracks were closing down after a fantastic season, surprisingly two circuits were opening up, and this in mid October! They were Leeds and Southampton. Leeds speedway held its first-ever meeting on October 14, and Eva Askquith was there as a spectator; she appeared in the role of a rider the week after! Although she won her heat in the Junior Handicap from the two second mark she found her grass track Velo not really a suitable machine for the dirt.

Dirt tracks built in stadiums intended for greyhound racing were, however, always at a disadvantage as compared with a circuit which had been specially constructed for the cinder game, because it was impossible to give the track anything other than long straights and short radius bends. The Leeds circuit (402 yards) was no exception; nevertheless it was a very fine track and drew weekly crowds of 10 - 12,000.

At that particular time Eva Askquith was employed in her father's butchery business in Bedale (Yorkshire) — the delivery girl you could call her, but besides taking out all the orders she used to bring in all the sheep and other beasts from neighbouring markets. Sometimes she walked the animals from Northallerton Auction Mart, some seven miles away, with just a stable lamp when cattle were purchased in the winter! There was no street lighting in the villages in those days. Yes, tough days indeed!

Leeds speedway opened again on March 30, 1929, and Eva was able to put in further appearances, but instead of using the old Velo it was now a proper dirt track Douglas, which suited her admirably with its very low frame, as Eva was not very tall, and had short legs.

It is interesting to note that no less than twenty three tracks were now operating Saturday meetings, like Leeds. They were: Barnsley, Birmingham, Bolton, Cardiff, Exeter, Glasgow, Leicester, Liverpool, Manchester's Belle Vue and White City, Nottingham, Rochdale, Sheffield, Southampton, Crystal Palace, Greenford, Harringay, King's Oak, Lea Bridge, Stamford Bridge, Warrington and Coventry. Several managements the previous year were staging two meetings per week, on Wednesdays and Saturdays! Such was the enthusiasm of dirt track racing.

The Yorkshire girl's initial races on her new Duggie, purchased entirely out of her prize money, were heat victories. A determined effort to alter things made her go faster and subsequent finals often saw her as the winner. She says: "I think the people in my home town of Bedale thought I was crackers in taking up this kind of sport, but all the same I put Bedale on the map."

After successes at the Rochdale and Middlesbrough tracks, and at various other Yorkshire circuits, Eva took her Douglas to Copenhagen in Denmark for a spell of racing, accompanied by riders George Reynard and Alex Jackson. Her riding caused a sensation. The Danes flocked to see this young lady of 23, who had the stamina and strength to hold a fast and heavy racing machine on a speedway and, what's more, to ride it at speeds that did her great credit.

The riders on that Copenhagen circuit were most spectacular and Miss Askquith simply had to go almost flat-out, cling on to her Duggie and hope for the best! It was not surprising that she met the "Great Dane", Morian Hansen, who was destined to ride for Hackney Wick and Wembley. He was an immensely tough fellow. There's many hair-raising stories of the Dane's determination, and his seeming indifference to hard knocks and pain.

It was no doubt that Eva Askquith's name created a record crowd of over 10,000 on her initial appearance. In her first race she defeated the two male riders opposed to her, after which came a few losses. However at the next meeting she had become more accustomed to the circuit and secured several more victories.

Incidentally, a giant trilby-hatted fellow always appeared at the Copenhagen meetings. He was the attendant Doctor named Ove Bevdixen, a very likeable and happy person, who tested all the riders' hearts before they started to race! "He was one of the greatest sports I have ever known," says Eva.

Returning to England after a very successful Danish tour, Miss Askquith found a heavy demand for her services and she raced on tracks as far apart as Glasgow, Exeter, Coventry and Wembley. At Leeds, her home track, the many enthusiasts welcomed her back with open arms — in fact the programme was headed: "WELCOME BACK, OUR EVA." And, apart from John Lloyd and Eric Langton on Rudges, every other rider was Douglas mounted.

To those who knew her closely, Eva Askquith was a most remarkable girl. Seeing her tearing round the speedways at around the 42mph mark gave everyone a complete sense of admiration and even more so when, at Gosforth, she defeated the Golden Helmet winner and record-breaker. It was a staggering feat. Then, to peep into her private life, it was difficult to recognise this Amazon of the Cinders in her reserved, sensitive and peace-loving nature.

Performing in front of a 17,000 crowd at Brough Park speedway, Eva won the first round of a match race against Gordon Byers, the 17 year old Newcastle Champion. Gordon won round two. Before the decider, the

Golden Helmet contest was staged and unfortunately for Eva she was involved in a triple crash sustaining a cut head which put her out of action for the remainder of the programme.

Undaunted by that nasty spill, Miss Askquith was racing again the next evening! This was at Gosforth speedway. The great "Smiling" Jim Kempster was there too as well as Charlie Barrett of Wembley, the fellow who before taking up the sport, practised by racing round a gasometer! His father happened to be the Gas Works manager in Devizes.

It must certainly be recorded that Eva rode in the victorious Leeds team against Sheffield at Owlerton on July 31, (1929). In one of her two rides as reserve she finished second in the fastest race of the evening. And Leeds won 35 - 28 points.

After winning a match race at the Crystal Palace at 42.41mph, Miss Askquith made her initial bow at Lea Bridge speedway in East London and broke the ladies' record by over five whole seconds. Her next engagements were three consecutive ones, at Wembley, West Ham and Southampton. Eva defeated Miss "Sunny Somerset" at the Empire Stadium. It was an easy victory but nevertheless a clever performance.

At West Ham she took on the Hammers captain, the formidable "Tiger" Stevenson and, although he had not yet reached the pinnacle of fame, he was, albeit, one of the best English riders. Eva won heat one of the match race at 38.38mph, but "Tiger" won round two at a slower speed. Now came the decider which Miss Askquith won by one length! It was a wonderful victory.

With her characteristic determination and courage she made her debut at Southampton. Her match race opponent? None other than the renowned "Sprouts" Elder. Needless to say, a tremendous crowd turned up. "Sprouts," the lean, lanky American was not only a star rider but a spectacular leg-trailer, and his Douglases, factory tuned, were some of the fastest in the country. He had things mostly his own way in the initial race, but Eva was never far behind. Race two saw her tearing round the track in the lead after a good start. "Sprouts" was playing his favourite cat and mouse game. His Duggie seemed to be cornering on its flywheel! But he left things a little too late, however, and misjudged Eva's speed. Putting on a tremendous spurt she went on to win in 82 seconds.

The two screaming Douglases echoed through the Banister Court Stadium. "Sprouts" had laid his machine over at an amazing angle in trying to catch his female opponent and overslid! It was now all level. Elder won the decider by two lengths.

The adventuresome spirit of Eva Askquith knew no bounds for, as the 1929 British season drew to an end we find her leaving for a spot of dirt track racing in Spain! The Spaniards gave her a rousing reception at Barcelona speedway, where she appeared several times. Then it was home again, and in a few months Eva sailed to South Africa to compete at Ellis Park speedway, Johannesburg where, on her first appearance a 15,000 crowd saw her in a match race against Joe Sarkis, the South African Champion. Over £1,000 was taken in gate money!

Back again in her Yorkshire home in April, 1930, Miss Askquith prepared for the English dirt track season. But her days in speedway were numbered. Vera Hole fell from her machine during a grand parade of riders and broke her collar-bone. This seemed sufficient excuse for the ACU to impose a restriction, and that fatal ban was implemented. Eva fought in vain against the decision and finally hung up her leathers. The ban was on in Britain but Eva was not deterred; she still yearned for the thrills of motorcycling. She returned to Spain in 1932, and acted as a picador on a motorcycle, with a matador as pillion passenger, in the bull rings at Barcelona, Madrid and at the Metropolitano Stadium! Other English riders, Charlie Barrett and Cliff Parkinson also took part.

Returning home once again, Eva went back to work and to attend to her father's Point-to-Point horses. When the war began she joined the National Fire Service as a dispatch rider, and was also a fire-engine driver.

Eva Askquith had, partly by common-sense and partly by good fortune, avoided the more serious of speedway accidents, but in 1959 came a most serious road accident. She was out on one of her meat delivery rounds when a car hit her van. Getting out to inspect the damage another car went straight into her. Poor Eva, with two broken legs and other injuries was taken to hospital where she remained for two years; and for a further two she had physiotherapy.

Over the years, Eva had become exceedingly interested in horticulture, so much so that she entered exhibits in various shows. She still does, even today, and great successes have come her way. Take for instance 1958, when she gained 21 firsts and two Trophies at the Ripon show. Since then she has won many other Trophies, medals and diplomas and first, second and third cards by the dozen. But today she has one big wish ... "I would love to meet Johnnie Hoskins once again" she says.

THE GIRLS certainly made a colourful and exciting short-term era·in dirt track racing, although their reign was all too brief. Nevertheless, their prodigious feats have never been forgotten by those who were fortunate enough to watch their exciting escapades on the Bristol-born blue and silver twins, those beautiful dirt track Duggies.

The baby of them all! Babs Neild poses

16 Lew Coffin

He's a familiar sight hurtling along on his 500cc JAP, in his blue and white leathers, blue crash helmet and white and red topped socks, generally ahead of a bunch of grass trackers. It's Lew Coffin, of course!

How many riders are still winning at the age of 54? The truth is there's only one. That's Lew, who has a status unique in the exciting world of speedway and grass track racing. Moreover he has enterprising plans already for this season, including several continental visits, which should dispel any ideas you might have that this pen portrait is by way of a swan song.

When a man of mature years says of himself: "I'm like that you know, impetuous and impulsive," it is possible to see why he can still hold his own with riders less than half his age!

Lew is, of course, the thoughtful, reliable, warm-hearted type of fellow, and he remains youngish in outlook, in health, and in his immense enthusiasm for motorcycles and motorcycling.

Normally his zestfulness is tempered by the wisdom of maturity, but occasionally, and not always at the wrong time, his underlying youthfulness will effervesce and he may then be accused of being impetuous.

Lew Coffin can justifiably boast of a total number of grass track victories far greater than any other rider in his thirty years of racing. Irrefutable statistics will prove it.

For the sheer love of grass track racing and of training potential grass track and speedway riders for the sake of the sport, you have to go a very long way to find anyone keener than veteran Lew, ex-speedway rider himself. Grass track racing has always stayed uppermost in his mind, but speedway has never been forgotten, and he has been intimately connected with Weymouth since it initially opened in 1954.

A regular performer at Bristol speedway in 1948, Lew's riding earned him the nickname of "The Killer!" He delighted the crowds with his neck-or-nothing style but the steward at one particular meeting reported him to the Control Board and he received the following letter from Major Fearnley.

"The Steward has drawn my attention to your riding at Bristol on June 25. In event six, in a fit of enthusiasm you bored one rider on the inside of one bend. On the next your riding carried another rider out to the safety fence, and after the Steward had switched on your exclusion light you ignored it and carried on, and on the next bend you knocked another rider off his machine, again from the inside. I must point out to you that if you are going to ignore the Steward's direction in this manner, then nothing but trouble can come of your behaviour. The Control Board is always glad to recognise enthusiasm in the right place, but you must watch your riding very carefully in future."

And so, daredevil Lew had to curb his reckless riding. Later in the year he was loaned to Exeter where he became a more stable competitor and secured a certain amount of success.

A wily master of track-craft, this Yeovil motor mechanic is an engaging character with an intense love of life. Lew is a stocky little fellow with broad shoulders, the result, no doubt, because he comes from farming stock, a circumstance which enabled him to ride home-made Bitzas in his father's fields at an early age.

Endowed with prodigious energy and common-sense, Lew has shouldered for most of his remarkable career, the exacting tasks of rider, mechanic, frame-builder and developer. The tuning side of things he has always left to Nelson Harring and his Harring-tuned JAP engined machines have carried him to a fantastic number of Championship and record-breaking successes at home and abroad.

On the track, great physical strength enables Lew Coffin to exploit his daring to a degree that might

The only picture taken of Lew Coffin, in 1964, with his superb collection of trophies. There are many more now!

otherwise be foolhardy and the crowds revel in his spectacular and forceful style. None of the stars he has left behind during his record 30 year racing period, has been at the top for so long and his illustrious achievements would be even more glittering, had he not had a share of bad luck, particularly in two Southern Centre Championships.

A true perfectionist, Lew builds his own racing machines, the notable, spotless, gleaming Lew Coffin Specials, in his workshops at Leigh, near Sherborne. He's also an inveterate champion of the underdog and is ever-helpful to fellow riders, the young ones in particular. He cheerfully puts aside his own interests to stand by a needy friend.

This "Dorset Flyer" has seen novices become stars and retire. He's raced against the sons of many riders who were once his rivals and he's seen many just fall by the wayside, for many are called but few are chosen. Speedway and grass tracking are both tough sports which, for some riders, so often leads to disillusionment instead of distinction.

Our elder statesman of the sport is one of those rare chaps who ploughs back into the racing game all the fun they have extracted from it, for he is a committee member of the Southern Centre Riders' Association, a founder member too, just twelve years ago. Not only that, but he is apt to pop up in all manner of guises ... as chief tutor for eight years at Weymouth speedway Training School ... as a sponsor, and as a speaker at the Club Dinner.

To be a grass tracker in the same class as the world's best you've got to get out and race against the world's best. Hence our star's excursion into National and Continental events. And, once you're at the top, he will tell you, the only way to stay there is to race regularly against the toughest opposition.

There are some riders who get ahead through sheer drive alone; others are lucky, but the Lew Coffin method is to apply in practical manner, sheer ingenuity, friendly co-operation, sound reasoning and a big handful of good humour.

To compete in one or more meetings every week-end calls for plenty of hard work and a lot of advance planning. Big distances have to be covered to race in a German International, usually a round trip of over a thousand miles. A few years ago Lew made no less than six such trips in one season! In 1973 he journeyed to the Osnabruck International meeting in Germany for his fifteenth successive time, a record in itself. This was not passed unnoticed by the promoting Club and a special presentation of an ornate Osnabruck Plate was made to him. In the process he had covered the best part of sixteen thousand miles!

Any meeting with Lew Coffin, no matter what the circumstances, is certain to be a pleasant one. For the style and determined dash and rugged toughness that he so superbly displays to such devastating effect in racing, conceals one of the most cheerful, harmless and frank dispositions with which any human has ever been endowed.

Lew and his wife Betty live in a bungalow in the Dorset village of Leigh, and in his spare time he's always to be found in his adjoining motorcycle workshops. A racing programme on the Coffin scale inevitably takes a substantial bite out of his working time, and Lew is thankful that his employer, his cousin Howard Coffin, has proved so amenable over the years.

The Half-Century Ace is, of course, chiefly renowned as a grass tracker and therefore his against the clock exploits in other forms of motorcycle sport only occupies an insignificant fraction of the time he has spent twisting the grips of the Lew Coffin Specials between 1945 and 1975, on the grass.

Speaking generally, Lew is of a quiet disposition. But when he buckles on his helmet appropriately emblazoned with a Union Jack; adjusts his goggles, puts on his gloves and straddles one of his LCS's, he becomes a changed character, for now he is a panther in disguise. When the contest is over, the battle won or lost, the ferocious, formidable Lew Coffin vanishes, and in his place we have your own likeable Lew back again.

Without doubt, this motorcycling star is a dedicated man; he's a thinker too and is blessed with other attributes that enable him to translate his thoughts into high speed two-wheel strategy. He has a profound knowledge of the mechanical side of racing and possesses the happy knack of being able to impart that knowledge to promising youngsters.

I have just said that Lew is a dedicated man. In fact he is more than that. Motorcycles are his whole world, virtually to the exclusion of all interests; he is rarely happy away from them. He approaches the task of racing with an almost fierce intensity of purpose, completely pre-occupied and almost oblivious to the flow of life around him. He loves a jostling tussle and has an almost incomprehensible sense of balance and throttle control, factors that mean that, when there is rain about, he thrills to the additional challenge a wet track provides and his broadsiding technique in such circumstances delights the crowds.

It was at the Southern Centre Championships in 1962 when three times in one afternoon the incredible happened. Lew was out to win all three category titles; it needed the greatest of efforts; it was a tremendous task. Notwithstanding, he accomplished this unique feat to become the first-ever Triple Champion, a super record that has never been equalled. His Centre too, appreciated his monumental achievements and he was presented with an additional trophy.

Lew returned to the speedway game again the following year when the Weymouth track re-opened and he was appointed Captain of the Royals. In his spare time he was at the track enthusiastically coaching the novices for he always had, and still has, the younger boys at heart.

In 1965 however, Lew won the Southern Centre Individual Championship for the seventh time and the sixth in succession, also the 350cc Championship for the fourth time; two records in themselves that have never been equalled. He also gained the South Western Centre Championship in the same season, a title that he has won several times since.

It was around the mid 'sixties that speedwaymen, Barry Briggs and Alf Hagon were challenging Lew's superiority on the grass. The races in which this trio of aces appeared, made grass track history and their exploits, particularly on the speedway-type oval circuit at Derriads Farm, near Chippenham, organised by the Wilts. Border Club for those fortunate enough to witness such magnificent racing, will certainly never be forgotten.

Fearless is an adjective that any conscientious biographer of Lew Coffin just has to use, simply because it so typically describes his riding. His tearaway, frighteningly fast into the bends technique makes him one of the most exciting to watch riders of the day. It is his natural style which could not be accentuated.

Out of action is anathema to his enthusiastic striving nature and riding at sometimes two or even three meetings a week, with the Continental trips thrown in, inevitably keeps him as busy as a big end. But the more he does, the better he's pleased! His trophies and medals, running into hundreds, portray an emblem of human endeavour. But he is more than a grass track ace. Many Clubs who have been treated to one of his informal talks, recognise him as a witty and gifted speaker.

Determination plus! '22' speeds onto yet another victory

Lew Coffin's greatest enemy today is Old Father Time, as racing on a scale like his must inevitably get harder as the years go by. Being diplomatic and by-passing him, I asked Betty, his wife, when she thought he was likely to pack it in. "I honestly have no idea" came her reply, "I don't really think he's ever given it a thought. Anyway, I wouldn't change our world for anything; seeing Lew happy is what really counts."

So what of the future? How much longer can the incredible Lew Coffin keep going? What is likely to force (and FORCE will certainly be the operative word) this great figure out of the game? These are really unanswerable questions. No doubt it will be old age in the end. But whatever the future holds it is a certainty that he will continue to be an integral part of grass track and speedway racing.

Where could we find his equal? Find anyone who has supported his beloved sports so faithfully? Thirty years in the grass track business and a big slice of it in the limelight is a fantastic record, apart from his speedway activities.

At the height of LEW COFFIN's career a friend of mine called him a Miracle Man. To me he will always be THE Miracle Man of grass track racing.

17 His ambition? ~ to be a professional speedway rider

Still growing; still shy; but once astride a racing machine he becomes a real star with the skill and the stamina of a veteran and each year bringing him fresh honours with greater fame. That is Sean Willmott from Willsbridge, near Bristol.

Initially for him, it was schoolboy scrambling in the Corsham Club events in which he shone with great brilliance, gaining most of the Championships and winning the Youth Motorcycle Schoolboys Association title when he was nine. Soon after, grass track racing claimed an additional and foremost interest and Sean, over the years, won practically every Championship in which he competed.

With enviable energy and enthusiasm he clinched the Junior Motorcycle Federation National Intermediate Championship for three consecutive seasons — a magnificent achievement, never beaten or even equalled. And the undisputed King of Schoolboy grass tracks was riding Tiger Cub and Honda machines (125ccs) both of which were built by his father John Willmott, a master engineer.

The vast crowds, the music, the floodlights, and everyone's eyes fixed on four speedway figures astride crackling machines at the starting gate. The music stops and you can, as it were, hear the silence, broken only by staccato exhaust notes. They're off! and the crowd roars ...

Certainly a stirring picture, and it's not surprising that many lads say; "I'd love to have a go at speedway racing." And so it was with Sean Willmott, but he was only ten at the time! Nevertheless Sean, with a suitable machine, attended the Weymouth speedway winter training sessions organised by tutor Lew Coffin and it was soon a common sight for the youngster to be scoring victories over some of his more-experienced seniors. Says Lew: "Sean is certainly a brilliant rider and his forceful style is a delight to watch; he has the professional speedway technique."

In 1974 however, Sean gained the Bristol Club's Grass Track Championship and won the Cotswold Club Championship for the third time. But in the '75 National Youth Senior Grass Track Championship it was a hard-luck story. His chain suddenly flew off in the semi-final when leading the race and the points score chart. Nevertheless the Bristol star took third overall position and was presented with an award donated by the Belle Vue speedway management. Sean was riding his new Moto-Vite, or in other words a "250" Maico engine in a cantilever frame.

Travelling great mileages pursuing his beloved sport, he races all over the country. Competing in one of his favourite areas, in Kent, he won the 200cc Kygstra British Championship.

Sean Willmott's great ambition is to be a professional speedway rider, and his past augurs well for it. But his father doesn't push him. Far from it. He prefers to let his son's progression take its natural course, and quite wisely so. His parents are, of course, proud of their son's motorcycling activities, and rightly so, for he is indeed worthy of that pride. Unassuming, happy-go-lucky youngsters like Sean certainly bring new life into the great family sport of ... speedway racing.

For a youngster to break into the speedway game today, times are undoubtedly tough, tougher than they have ever been. The extremely high cost of machinery, leathers, spares, helmet, etc., makes it that way, unfortunately. But Sean is determined that nothing will put him off. He has started young, very young. Even now he is only 14 years old, but has been racing since he was 5½!

Despite all the honours that have come Sean's way, and they are vast in number, he still remains an exceptionally quiet and modest lad, with courage and determination too, all of which sums up his outstanding characteristics.

Fourteen-year-old Sean Willmott at Weymouth Speedway, 1975. Sean, on his newly acquired 500cc Jawa, shows his tremendous aptitude for the sport

The lad's racing future seems assuredly bright, and brighter still, now that the Shaleway Chiefs are at last taking an interest in schoolboy grass track racing, the British Speedway Promoters' Association having donated three trophies for its Championship meeting. They know only too well that their future stars will inevitably come from the schoolboys, who are now participating in this other branch of the motorcycle sport.

So Sean Willmott's aim is to be a full-time speedway rider. Judging by his past performances on a smartly styled and indisputably attractive 250cc BSA at Weymouth speedway and now with a 500cc Jawa given to him by his very generous father ... he's more than half-way there!

Sean Willmott's already handsome collection of trophies, some of them won at grass track events. Remember he is still only fourteen-years-old

18 Test Matches: England versus Australia

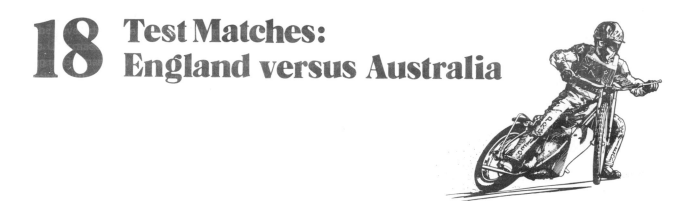

That small band of Australian riders who came to England in 1928, became the pioneers, as far as the great body of our public was concerned, of a new and exciting sport called dirt track racing. They had nicknames supposed to be suggestive of the particular characteristics of each rider — "Broadside" Vic Huxley, "Wizard" Frank Arthur and "Cyclone" Billy Lamont to name but a few. They amazed everyone, (including those English motorcyclists who became converts to the new mode of progression round a small track), by their uncanny skill and apparently reckless disregard for their own safety.

Towards the end of that first season, one or two Englishmen who had made more rapid progress than the others, had become so good that the time was even then envisaged when English riders would meet the renowned Australians on level terms.

In 1930, the progress was maintained, and although a few of the Australians were so outstandingly brilliant that they could still fairly claim to be on top, it became a matter of controversy what would happen if the best of them were confronted by a representative English side.

It was however, decided to put the matter, literally, to the test. The inaugural Test Match took place at the Wimbledon track on June 30, 1930, before a crowd which filled the stadium to the utmost capacity. Opinions had differed as to the respective prospects, but England's heavy defeat, by 35 points to 17, in a six-a-side contest came as a sensation. For Australia, Vic Huxley scored the full nine points; Frank Arthur and Billy Lamont and Max Grosskreutz six each and Ron Johnson, five.

After this however, the matches were contested over sixteen heats. Whether or not this was to the disadvantage of the Australians, who naturally had fewer potential Test riders, was a moot point. Certainly it was that England, despite various mishaps, won a most creditable victory at Belle Vue in that season's second Test, thanks largely to Jim Kempster and "Squib" Burton, despite the twelve-point score of Grosskreutz. England won also the other remaining three matches, including a memorable one at Stamford Bridge, when a huge crowd waited patiently for half an hour in total darkness. The floodlights had failed in the middle of the programme!

In 1931 England won four matches ... and the Test crowds grew bigger and bigger: 84,000 at the first Test at Wembley in 1932!

The English side routed the Australians at the Crystal Palace for the first Test of 1931; Australia won in that disastrous second match at Leicester, when Wal Phillips, the English captain and "Squib" Burton were seriously injured, and England came very near indeed to victory in the fifth match at Stamford Bridge, when Frank Arthur seemed to be heading for a last-heat win, only to sustain mechanical trouble, an almost unheard of thing for the best-equipped rider in the game. In that match it was undoubtedly Jack Parker's brilliance, (he was unbeaten and unbeatable) that turned the scales in favour of the home country.

These super Test Matches were, without doubt, the high-spots of speedway racing, which aroused terrific enthusiasm and drew immense crowds. With the top aces of both countries fighting for supremacy in an annual series of five matches, racing was invariably of the highest order. The very mention of Test contests sent the blood surging through the veins in a warm tingle of anticipation.

After a lapse from 1953 to 1969 the long-standing England v. Australia Test Match series were revived in 1970, but they were conspicuously absent from the 1971 events. In the previous year three matches unfortunately had to be cancelled owing to bad weather, and it seemed a shame that the attempt to revive speedway's oldest

The first England Test Team to visit Australia. From left to right; *Joe Abbott, Wal Phillips, Tiger Stevenson, Frank Varey, Herbert Haigh and Cliff Parkinson*

The Australian Test Team at Belle Vue in 1930, with live kangaroo too! From left to right; *Billy Lamont, Buzz Hibberd, Frank Arthur, Jack Chapman (almost hidden), Ron Johnson (who moved), Dicky Case, Dicky Wise, Max Grosskreutz and Vic Huxley*

The England Test Team (Third Test) in 1951. From left to right; Top row, *Freddie Williams, Tommy Price, Ronnie Greene (manager), Jack Parker* and *Cyril Roger.* Bottom row; *George Wilks, Split Waterman, the late Alan Hunt* and *Norman Parker*

New Cross 1949, the Australian Test Team. From left to right; Top row, *the late Ray Duggan, Ron Johnson, Bill Longley* and *Ken Le Breton.* Bottom row, *Aub Lawson, Arthur Payne, Arthur Simcock (manager), Cliff Watson* and *Graham Warren*

One of the greatest leg-trailers of all time, the courageous George Newton, getting into trouble at Newcastle Speedway

International series was doomed to failure. The contributory reason was, of course, the inability of the Australians to form a crowd-pulling side, that would be capable of holding its own on the English First Division circuits.

This is a far cry indeed from the first post-war Test series in 1948 for instance, when a five-match series attracted an incredible 124,000 enthusiasts; at Wimbledon 22,000; Harringay 29,000; Belle Vue 20,000; New Cross 21,000 and West Ham 32,000.

The highlight however, of that season's contests was the sensational introduction of the incomparable 22 year old blonde Australian, Graham Warren, whose brilliance put him in a class of his own. He achieved Test Match ambitions in his first season of English racing. Dynamic Graham was a member of the Birmingham side, truly the shock team of the year and the one that set everyone talking after his brilliant performance in the final Test at West Ham — then Britain's fastest track. He proved a rich reward for the astuteness of promoter Les Marshall in signing the star-to-be after seeing his performance in a few trial laps. The Wimbledon management made the fantastic offer of £4,000 for his services! But Birmingham would not part.

Since that first-ever match in 1930, a total of nearly a hundred have been decided and the supreme individual top-scorer is Jack Parker who amassed an incredible 460 points. Second comes Max Grosskreutz (374) and third, the late "Bluey" Wilkinson with 359.

The classic England v. Australia Test Matches remained the show pieces of the season and although the contests with other countries over the years have tended to diminish their glory, nothing can take away the glamour of those great International clashes ... the most famous of them all.

Kangaroo versus Lion, the renowned Vic Duggan in front of Jack Parker

19 The World Championship through the years

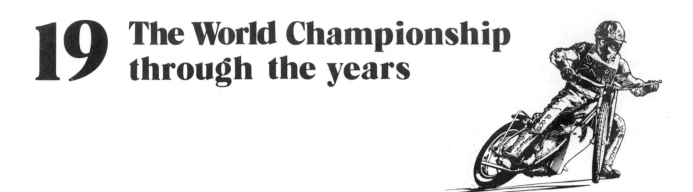

CHAMPION OF THE WORLD! What an impressive title that is, and no wonder that the top-flight riders devote so much of their summer season to making hurried journeys all over Europe in the search for points which may, eventually, earn them the title of World Speedway Champion.

Out of hundreds of riders, only sixteen are eligible for the Final each year, and the struggle is certainly a stern one. No flash in the pan brilliance will win one of the titles, for qualifying rounds are spread over a period of many months, and the would-be champion must be consistent as well as capable.

The history of the World Championships is a long one. 1936 saw the first official Championship to be recognised as such by the FICM (the Federation Internationale des Clubs Motorcyclistes) the international controlling body of all motorcycle sport which now operates under the initials FIM. But the story really begins much earlier, actually in 1929, when the Star Championship was acknowledged as speedway's greatest event. With its galaxy of star riders, the competition was, virtually, a World Championship, in which all the crack riders competed each year for the trophy and cash awards, until the last of the series which ended in 1935.

To assist a clean and wholesome sport and one that depended as, of course, it still does, for its popularity not on betting but on its intrinsic worth, the proprietors of *The Star,* the London evening newspaper, offered the Association of Motorcycle Track Racing Promoters a prize of £250 cash and a £50 Trophy to the winner of the Home Section and also the Overseas Section. Roger Frogley and Frank Arthur were the respective victors in that inaugural contest.

1930 came round when the two separate competitions were amalgamated. Vic Huxley was the winner that season, followed by Ray Tauser, Eric Langton, Tom Farndon, Jack Parker and Frank Charles respectively for the remaining five seasons.

Frank Charles, the '35 Star Champion (sadly killed in a gliding accident in 1939) gave a brilliant display of riding and his victory was all the more gratifying to Wembley supporters because he was the first Lion to secure the coveted title. And, by also gaining the Wembley Gold Cup Championship, and then the Wembley Grand Prix, Frank earned for himself the title of the Greatest Rider of the Year. Incidentally, in the Wembley Grand Prix he won a brand new Martin JAP speedway machine. Its value then is interesting today. Just £80!

So ambitious was the scale on which the first Championship had been planned that the total prize money involved the enormous sum of £3,536. The entire Wembley circuit had been torn up and the foundations re-laid, especially for the great event; several hundred tons of cinders were used to cover the track to a depth of four inches. The best was only good enough for Sir Arthur Elvin.

75,000 enthusiasts watched the 27 year old Australian, Lionel Van Praag, gain 26 points in that history-making Final, and Sir Malcolm Campbell, then the fastest man in the world on land, presented a cinder-grimed Lionel with the Championship trophy and a £500 cheque. He had beaten Eric Langton in a dramatic and thrilling run-off ... he was number-one in an illustrious line of the famous. But "Bluey" Wilkinson had scored victories over every opponent in turn; he accomplished the seemingly impossible feat of beating Langton and Van Praag in successive races. It was the riding of a champion. But the controversial bonus points system in the qualifying rounds had relegated him to third place. It was however, significant that he received the biggest cheers of the entire evening.

In the following year's Final there was an increased attendance of 10,000 over the '36 figure and the

The Australian, Lionel Van Praag, the first World Champion under the FIM in 1936

"Bluey" Wilkinson — World Champion in 1938

Americans completely dominated the event to such an extent that they filled the first three places. Jack Milne, the top qualifier and one of the illustrious figures to wear the orange and black of the New Cross Rangers, scored a maximum to become a clear-cut winner. Runner-up was Wilbur Lamoreaux, and in third place came Cordy Milne, Jack's brother.

1938, and a record-breaking 90,000 saw the gallant Arthur Wilkinson, West Ham's terrier-like Australian, known affectionately to all his friends as "Bluey", emerge as World Champion. Previously, in his home country, he had swept the board at most of the important meetings. It was his big season in England too; at West Ham he was practically invincible and won a host of trophies. But only great determination had given him the coveted title, for he was racing with injuries. The previous evening at New Cross in a spill he received concussion and damaged his shoulder. Despite the pain of this, his shoulder was strapped up and he battled through to World Championship victory amid one of the greatest receptions ever given to a rider. Jack Milne and Wilbur Lamoreaux filled second and third spots respectively.

It was a great disappointment to the Wembley management who were forced, owing to the outbreak of World War Two, to cancel the 1939 Final as they had made room for 106,000 people. It was no less a disappointment to the Southampton team-man, Cordy Milne, the rider who had the biggest chance of taking the title as top qualifier. But perhaps he gained some consolation in the fact that he immediately went to Australia and won that country's speedway Championship for 1940.

With speedway racing being resumed on a National scale in 1946, the British Riders' Championship replaced the World Championship for three successive seasons. That controversial bonus points system was abolished and every rider started on level terms. The winners were: Tommy Price, 1946; Jack Parker, 1947 and, the sensational, Vic Duggan in 1948. For the first time in the history of the competition, a member of the Royal Family, H.R.H. the Duke of Edinburgh, presented the Trophy and cash award to a gleaming Australian, Vic Duggan, in '48. The New Cross idol, Ron Johnson, was runner-up, with Alec Statham in third spot.

The first English World Champion came in 1949. It was Wembley's own Tommy Price who received the beautiful *Sunday Dispatch* Trophy; it was a new Trophy, a shorter and plumper one, that replaced the magnificent tall and slender Cup that had been awarded in pre-war years.

The 1950 Finalists were a wonderful blend of youth and experience. There was Tasmanian-born Ronnie Moore, earning in the region of £500 a month by his riding skill, and at the tender age of 17 was the youngest rider ever to appear in a World Final. Then there was Jack Young, the Edinburgh skipper in Division Two, who burst into big-time racing by heading the list of qualifiers. "Split" Waterman was there too and fiery Graham Warren. But it was the 24 year old Welshman, Freddie Williams, watched by his mother and father, who gave Wembley its third World Champion. Practically unknown before 1948, he proved a most surprising winner. Surprise too was runner-up 28 year old, battle scarred, Wally Green.

Jack Young blasted his way to another victorious finish in 1952 to become the first double Champion. He was then faced with a tremendous task; an ambition to become triple Champion in 1953. But for Jack, Lady Luck failed to smile upon him, as track conditions were not in his favour and he came in fifth. It was Freddie Williams who gained the title for the second time.

Every year brought its surprises in the top end of the Final. In 1954 three important new youngsters appeared for the first time, and three newcomers were each to become World Champion. Peter Craven in 1955, Ove Fundin in '56 and Barry Briggs in '57. But, for the '54 contest Ronnie Moore proved the winner. He left no doubt in the minds of the 90,000 crowd that he was Champion of Champions. The wildly excited fans rose to him in one stupendous, deafening roar. His victory had been clear-cut and decisive ... five rides, five wins was the hallmark of a great and worthy Champion.

The 1958 Final had a new look, as the *Sunday Pictorial* were the new sponsors and had donated a brand new Trophy that had been designed specially for the event. Unbeaten in his five rides, Barry Briggs retained his Title and therefore became the second rider in Championship history to gain the honour two years in succession.

With winners Ronnie Moore in 1959 and Ove Fundin, the Swedish Champion, in '60, there came a change of venue in '61 from Wembley, after a continuous run of fifteen years, to Malmo in Sweden. And, once again, it was the dynamic Ove Fundin, the European and Nordic Champion, who in retaining the World Championship became the first-ever rider to win the competition three times.

Malmo's 440 yard red shale track proved the downfall of the British contingent of nine. The massive crowd roared its appreciation to Ove Fundin, the triple speedway King, and acknowledged him as the greatest-ever Champion. It was also a tremendous achievement for British JAP engines, the machines of which had filled the first three places.

It all depends on the start! Graham Warren (left), *then Split Waterman, Ronnie Moore and Jack Parker* (right) *line up for the fourth race in the 1950 World Championship final*

The fastest man on water, the late Donald Campbell CBE presents Barry Briggs with the massive World Championship Trophy in 1958

The first Russian to race in England, 29 year old Igor Plechanov, made his debut in Wembley's 1962 Final. He scored one brilliant first and four fighting thirds, and his tenth place caused more than a slight stir on the speedway front. The magnificent riding of Peter Craven, with his unique style giving the full thrill of flat-out broadsiding, gave him the World Crown for the second time and the Belle Vue skipper took tenth place in the following year's event, won by Fundin, who courageously rode with broken ankle-bones still in plaster. But, sad to say, it was Peter's last World Final. Just ten days after, he was tragically killed at Edinburgh, and the speedway world mourned the loss of an outstanding and remarkable youngster.

Ullevi speedway, at Gothenburgh in Sweden, was chosen for the 1964 contest and the New Zealander, Barry Briggs, on the top of his form, was unbeaten in five wet rides. His 2-point victory over Igor Plechnov delighted the half thousand British fans who had flown over. Thus Barry became the second only rider to win the Title more than twice.

It was back again to Wembley in '65 and Briggs, the British Champion, was the favourite once again ... but on the big night he rode disappointingly; his Eso seemed to lack speed on a track made heavy by early afternoon rain.

JAP engined riders were heavily outnumbered by the Eso competitors but Bjorn Knutsson scored a JAP engine victory. World motor racing Champion Jim Clark, tragically killed two and a half years later, presented the Trophy to Bjorn and the valiant Swede returned to his home country and to his Norrkoping car business, £600 the richer.

1974. The World Final at Gothenburg. Anders Michanek, the winner, with Ivan Mauger (second) *and Soren Sjosten* (third) *on the right of the photograph*

1975. The World Final at Wembley. "White line man" Peter Collins inside John Louis and Henryn Glucklich

1966, and everything was all set for the 21st World Championship Final. For the second time it was staged at Ullevi stadium and in five unbeaten rides 32 year old Barry Briggs, appearing in his thirteenth Final, gained the Title for the fourth time. It was the Eso machine's initial Title win, but Barry's victory was all the more meritorious as his shoulder was still bound up from an injury received in a German grass track meeting.

Speedway racing received a terrific booster when, in the following year, the sponsors doubled the winner's prize money to a staggering £1,000. This made the Final one of the richest of all motorcycle racing events. On that evening at Wembley Ove Fundin (JAP) proved the world's best for the fifth time as the 34 year old Swedish veteran defeated his compatriot, Bengt Jansson, the pride of Hackney Wick, in the decider. Bengt was riding an Eso with a Wal Phillips fuel injector attached and Wal was certainly a delighted fellow that particular evening. And Ove earned almost £1,100 in six minutes riding!

For the next five years (1968-72) the Final was dominated by the fellow who was destined to become a grass track ace, the renowned Ivan Mauger, apart, of course, from the '71 event won by Ole Olsen with Ivan taking second spot. Mauger therefore, was the first-ever rider to win three consecutive Titles.

Incredible. That was really the only word to describe the 1973 event when for the first time in its history the Title went behind the Iron Curtain as Jerzy Szckakiel, an almost unknown 22 year old, became Poland's first World Speedway Champion before a delirious, near 100,000 crowd at the Slaski Stadium, Katowice, Poland. Completely unfancied, the fiery Jerzy grabbed the Title from the holder, Ivan Mauger in a sensational run-off as the New Zealander clipped his opponent's back wheel and was flung over his handlebars. The other Polish ace, Zenon Plech gained third spot.

With meteor-like starts and beaten only once into the first corner, 31 year old Anders Michanek from Stockholm made five perfect rides that had a record crowd of 40,000 wild with delight at the Ullevi Stadium, Gothenburg, giving Sweden its first World Champion for seven years. And to prove he was the complete master, Anders broke the track record three times! In that 1974 World Final the cool, calm and confident Swede made his 15 rivals look like also-rans as he claimed victory in each of his races.

"I'm on the top of the world," exclaimed Ole Olsen as he revelled in his meritorious victory at Wembley in the '75 World Championship Final. Unbeaten, his 15 points flowed from five super starts and, in his own immaculate style, he was never headed. And, while he was in the process of gaining his second World Title, his fifteen opponents got themselves into all sorts of trouble on a very poorly-prepared and bumpy track. The state of the circuit caused tremendous controversy.

But after-meeting celebrations were short indeed for the illustrious and ambitious Dane, as he flew out, later the same evening, to fulfil a racing engagement on the following day in Denmark.

After thirty World Championship Finals (1936-75), comes the time to sum up the Supreme World Finalist. And that goes to the legendary Swede, Ove Fundin, with five victories, three seconds and three thirds; a superb record that has never been beaten or even equalled. He made thirteen World Championship appearances; won the European Championship five times, the Swedish Championship five times and the Nordic Championship in '61, whilst his English successes included the Match-Race holder during eight years, and the Internationale winner three times.

20 Speedway - on spikes

Speedway racing on ice! Undoubtedly it's the world's most ferocious and dangerous sport and a sport reserved for the brave ... a sport which for sheer spectacle cannot be surpassed. And the men who take part in it are the real tough-nuts of the motorcycle brigade.

Sweden was originally the real home of ice racing and in the mid 'fifties Thord Larsson was the ace of the ice racers. He joined Folke Mannersted in the production of the SRM and HRM speedway engines and these, of 497cc capacity were not unlike the speedway JAP in appearance.

Larsson who lives in Stockholm, clocked an average speed of 60mph, on the local 1,000 metre cinder surface and 75mph on ice, with an HRM. And this was over 25 years ago! At that particular time the majority of riders rode British JAP machines, but today, as in shale speedway, the riders are usually on Jawas.

Unlike the Russian ace, the seasoned campaigner Gad Kadyrov, the most successful rider in the sport, who has gained six World Championships in eight years, others such as Graham Miles, Bruce Semmens, Barry Briggs, Ove Fundin, Malcolm Simmons, Joe Hughes, Bruce Cribb, Richard Greer, Goog Allen and Ivan Mauger, comparatively speaking, have only flitted across the ice racing scene, although they all made an impression.

However, Britain's first-ever world ice racing finalist was Andy Ross who finished a joint tenth in the 1969 event at Inzell in the Bavarian Alps, after two spectacular crashes. "I've ridden my last ice race, now that I've reached my ambition of competing in a World Final" he remarked.

But surprisingly, the Scottish-born British Grass Track Champion of 1968 (500cc class) came back for more. In the 1970 World Ice Contest he again reached the Final which took place on a 300 yard mini-circuit at Nassjo in Southern Sweden. Andy brilliantly gained a joint-fifth place, and through this achievement he still holds the title of the best-ever British performer on Europe's awe-inspiring ice tracks.

And this was definitely Andy's final fling. "Those who ride the ice must be mad" he later exclaimed, against himself. And who could blame him? He had already been "spiked" the length of his back!

That World Championship Final in 1970 however was won by the Czech veteran, Antonin Svab, a 37 year old rider who worked in the Jawa factory. He scored a 15 point maximum to oust the Russian riders from top place for the first time since the series began in 1966. Today, Antonin (the Czech speedway champion in 1967 and 1968) works in England; he is Skoda's Technical Services Manager at Kings Lynn.

Antonin, tremendously courageous, like all the rest, secured second spot in the World Championship in 1972, despite three heavy falls. Previously in the 1969 Final at Inzell's 400 metre track in West Germany and watched by 15,000 tightly-packed spectators, Svab crashed in a last-lap, death or glory challenge with Vladimir Zibrov, the previous year's Russian National Champion. His rear wheel spikes ripped into his heel bone, tearing the achilles tendon and poor Antonin was hospitalised for the next six months. He was however, warned by his Doctor never to race again but the determined Czech still yearned to race and competed in a grass meeting near Frankfurt. Ahead of the pack in his initial race, he suddenly came off. Closely following was a Norwegian rider who ran over his leg, breaking his ankle; then a Swede hit his head and the unfortunate Svab sustained a four inch fracture of the skull and a two inch crack in his temple.

Antonin lay unconscious in hospital for three whole days. A month later he returned home. Miraculously, just six months after that serious grass track accident, the super-brave Czech clinched his World Ice Championship title.

The ferocious looking ice-racer with 90 inch-long spikes on its front wheel and 200 on its rear!

On one particular occasion Antonin Svab, a keep-fit addict, raced in a temperature of no less than forty seven degrees below zero! This was at the Prokopevsk ice circuit in Siberia. Several weeks earlier he had been the victim of a nasty eye injury and during a race at Prokopevsk, tears from the eye started running down his cheek. Then suddenly he lost the sight of it and after an examination in hospital it was found to be frozen solid! But things ended on a happier note when the courageous Czech later regained his sight, which at one time was thought to be lost for ever.

Like conventional speedway, events are run on oval ice circuits, usually about 440 yards round. Clutch starts are used and four riders (it used to be limited to three) partake in 4-lap races run anti-clockwise. But there the similarities come to an end, apart, of course, from the old-time leg-trailing technique.

Ice racing machines are fearful looking objects. Their most impressive feature is the inch long vicious-looking steel spikes which adorn both wheels, 90 on the front tyre and 200 on the rear. They have been screwed into treadless tyres, and provide fantastic grip. With super traction such as this, two-speed gearboxes are a necessity and with fifty brake horse power beneath them, the riders are usually mono-wheeling just after the start and change gear with the front wheel still pawing the air!

Of course, broadsiding is non-existent and machines are banked over at alarming angles, in fact clutch levers and handlebars just skim the ice surface.

These lethal spikes, the riders will tell you, are their worst enemy. They can do enormous damage. With speeds of up to 80mph, on the straights, and 60mph on the corners, if a rider is unlucky enough to fall, those whizzing spikes can slice through boots or leathers like a knife through butter. Even so, these intrepid and admirable gladiators seem to be worry-free, and bumping and boring is not uncommon.

Joe Hughes, the English star, takes a nasty-looking tumble in front of Zdanek Kudrna (Czech) in Moscow's Dynamo Stadium

The ice racing model has a long wheelbase and a more stable and rigid frame as compared to the conventional speedway machine. Its wheels are equipped with special protective guards, mudguard style, which are compulsory, and which reach almost to the surface of the ice. Handlebars are low-slung for the exclusive leg-trailing style and a damper keeps the steering quite rigid.

Sub-zero temperatures however, present some technical problems, such as that of starting the machines. Normally, riders heat the oil before filling their tanks, which are installed close to the cylinder barrel. A blow lamp or other form of heating is directed over the engines to warm them up for staring and the riders bind a section of a car or motorcycle tyre to their heavily padded left legs, which are in constant contact with the surface of the ice. Banked-up snow and ice form the only safety-fence!

The origins of this super-exciting sport seem rather blurred, but an ice racing event was staged in Germany as early as 1925 and this took place on the frozen Eibsee, a lake near Garmisch-Partenkirchen. As the early 1930's came round the sport was spreading its wings, and meetings on many Bavarian lakes, became very popular, as well as in Scandinavia and Canada.

Unfortunately World War Two began and racing stopped. When hostilities ended, the Scandinavians were the first in the field in reviving the so-called 'Killer' sport.

The enthusiastic Russians, who have now been fostering the game for over a quarter of a century, then took the lead, and have dominated it ever since. They were successful in persuading the FIM (the world's governing body of motorcycle sport) to institute European Championships in 1963. Three years later came the World events. Thus in 1966, Speedway Ice Racing was installed as a World Championship sport.

The first three Championship Finals were staged in Russia and the fourth at Inzell (West Germany). Since then two further Finals have had Inzell as their venues; three have been held at Nassjo in Sweden and one at Moscow.

Sergey Tarabanko (USSR) 1976 World Champion here at Assen during one of his winning rides

Of the popularity of the sport there is no doubt. Take for instance the semi-final event at Inzell in 1972 when 5,000 were locked out because of a capacity crowd! The eager enthusiasts at a semi-final or final meeting, pack the stands and terraces up to five hours before the start, and endure below freezing conditions just for an assurance of their places.

Another of Russia's great ice warriors, a breed of iron-nerved men, is Boris Samorodov who has held his country's National Ice Racing title on more than one occasion. It was Boris who took the World Title in 1967 and he will certainly be remembered for a sensational World speedway Final at Wembley in 1963. Even at forty two years of age, he came close to achieving his second World Ice Title in the Final at Inzell in '74 but a rather horrific crash ended his high hopes. The Czech, Jan Verner came to grief on a bend where the natural ice was thawing and Samorodov, right on his heels, unavoidably, ran over Jan's legs amid showers of ice chippings. Rushed to hospital the unfortunate Czech was sewn up with forty stitches.

The event however, produced a win for the 23 year old Milan Spinka, a short stocky Czechoslovakian policeman, and better known in England as a top member of the Czech's conventional speedway squad that had previously made appearances on Division Two circuits. In five scintillating rides, gaining victories from the front and from the back, Milan gained a fifteen point maximum. Nobody could beat him, not even the Russian aces, Zybrov, Kadyrov and Tarabanko who came in second, third and fourth respectively and Spinka's incredible form won for him the handsome World Trophy, at the Nassjo Ice Rink, Sweden, on March 9.

"Spike King" Spinka's skills had not only been highlighted in Ice Racing, for, in the previous year he qualified for the World Thousand Metre Sand Track Final in Oslo. Notching ninth spot was exceedingly good when one considered the formidable opposition, former World Speedway Champion Ole Olsen, the West German national long track Champion Hans Siegl, and the notable Manfred Poschenrieder. But Spinka's ice racing reign lasted just one year, for the 1975 World Title was gained by Sergei Tarabanko, the 25 year old Russian sports teacher, who went through the two-day meeting at the Dynamo Stadium in Moscow, unbeaten. The Russians really dominated the event, taking the first six places.

A study in ice cold concentration, Vladimir Smirnov (USSR) follows Jan Verner (Czech) during the 1976 Assen World Championship final

The Final, however, was witnessed by a record crowd of over 100,000, who watched the men with a special brand of courage dicing it out on ice. The former Russian trainer Samorodov had been replaced by six times World Ice Racing Champion, Gab Kadyrov, and the winner Tarabanko from Novosibirsk was also trained by him.

There is no doubt that the ice stars seem to have a certain character about them. They create atmosphere; they make sure the fans know they are top men in a very dangerous sport; they are clever and their names have a personality ring around them. These heroic riders with an insatiable thirst for speed, on ice, are certainly to be marvelled at.

Will ice racing ever be staged in Britain? I have my doubts. Indoor stadiums are far too small. To flood and freeze speedway circuits, like the artificially created ice track at Inzell, would present enormous costs, and this would certainly not be the only problem.

21 Superstars - ten of the best

MALCOLM SIMMONS

100mph? No, it is certainly not seen in speedway racing, but occasionally it shows itself on a big grass track circuit. Hitting the magic ton along the straights in the '65 National ACU Star competition at Stokenchurch (Bucks) were the speed kings, Malcolm Simmons, Don Godden and Tony Black, all on JAP engined machines. And, 19 year old Malcolm, on the 1,400 yard course, defeated these two deadly rivals in the 350 Star event. When leading them in the 1,000cc race by 20 yards he retired, after his exhaust pipe had come adrift.

It was, however the last blow of a very expensive weekend's racing and, frustratingly, he set off to see the evening meeting at Wembley speedway!

But Malcolm was no newcomer to grass track racing. He had actually started at the early age of 15, in '61, and was voted the best young rider of the season at the Maidstone Aces Club's meetings. Two years later he was right at the top and a real ace. Once astride one of his Hagon JAPs he became a real giant-killer with the skill and the stamina of a veteran, amazing the crowds by beating his older, more-experienced rivals. Christened the "Teenage Terror", each season brought him fresh honours with greater fame. And at the same time he was establishing himself as a speedway rider with Hackney. But it took him ten years to really leave the shadows and come into the limelight as the "Golden Boy" of speedway. "I had only been playing with speedway until '73" he freely admits. "Then I took things more seriously but through all those years I had been living and learning" he adds with a smile.

Blonde Malcolm deservedly secured a regular berth in the England speedway team and a World Team Cup Gold Medal (for the part he played in three consecutive British successes), which made life even rosier for the lad from Rainham, in Kent, who, incidentally, goes trials riding in the winter.

After a period with West Ham, he joined the King's Lynn team in '68; several years later he amassed a superb score of 400 points in one season, to become top man at Saddlebow Road. Gaining the '74 Spring Classic event he then joined Poole in '75 and later made his first-ever World Championship Final appearance in which he won a meritorious joint fifth place.

In retrospect, 1965 was a fantastic grass track season, for teenager Simmons's successes flew off his rear wheel like clockwork monotony. Running through a host of meetings absolutely undefeated, he won, for the second time, the South Eastern Centre Championship and again for the second time was voted South Eastern Riders' Association's Personality of the Year. Trounching the National Champion, Alf Hagon, in several Match Races, Malcolm gained a creditable third place in the 350 National Championships, a similar place to which he had occupied the previous year.

Scoring its seventh win in the 17 year old Inter-Centre Championships, the South Eastern Centre snatched back the solo crown from the reigning Midland Centre Champions in '67 at Berwick St. Leonard in Wiltshire. And Malcolm was a member of the famous and victorious team.

That particular afternoon I saw one of the greatest races I had ever seen in my long association with the sport. It was the first leg for the five-hundreds. Malcolm, on an Eso, rocketed ahead, with Lew Coffin (LCS JAP) hot on his heels. But Lew, then 45 years old, soon ousted the young "Blonde Hammer" from his slender lead at the end of lap one. From then on, with Peter Randall (Hagon JAP) joining in the tussle, the three aces fought a titanic battle which ended in Lew, Malcolm and Peter, flashing over the finishing line in that order, with just a few inches separating all three.

That's a race I'll always remember!

PETER COLLINS

Peter Collins became a Champion at 17! And this was in the '71 British Grass Track Championship (350 class) on his Hagon JAP, when the Rochdale teamster quenched a long-odds challenge from Tig Perry, to become the youngest-ever title holder. And he also shocked the 250cc and 500cc contenders as well.

Once again he won the 350 title in the following season, his spectacular full-blooded style, bringing thousands from all over the country to see him race. Superb, incredible, stupendous, breathtaking ... these were just a few of the superlatives used in describing his fantastic riding.

Out of his neat blue leathers and crash helmet, both liberally splashed with coloured stars, the renowned teenager would never be recognised as the lad who had been setting the circuits alight with his gravity-defying technique.

When Peter clinched his grass track title in '71, it was less than a year since his first ever race on a 250. But he had been riding bikes ever since he was eight, around his father's farm field near Lymm in Cheshire. With his long track Jawa, in front of a 12,000 crowd, he kept Anders Michanek and Ivan Mauger at bay to win the International Race of the Aces race at Beeford.

1973 saw him as a fully professional and he had also been carving out an equally successful speedway career with Belle Vue. The clash of speedway interests unfortunately kept him out of the British Grass Track Championships and in the end, grass track's loss was speedway's gain.

Throughout the '73 season the name of Peter Collins dominated the speedway headlines. One of his most meritorious performances was in the Knock-out Cup contest Final which he virtually won for Belle Vue. Acclaimed as the hero of the evening, the ever-cheerful, wavy-haired Peter was riding with a cracked left wrist in protective casing. He had switched the clutch lever to the throttle side of his handlebars! And yet, riding in this unconventional fashion produced a match-winning final ride over Michanek.

In his typical dynamic style, Peter had previously won the British Junior Speedway Championship and not long after his knock-out triumph he set sail for Australia as a member of the British Touring Team. His high contributory number of points enabled a brilliant side to win the Ashes.

Peter ended the '75 season in a blaze of glory and retained his British League Riders' Championship title with a dazzling display of brilliancy. Previously in the World Final at Wembley, he had taken a creditable joint fifth place. In the important World Team Cup Final held at Norden, West Germany, he was a member of the highly successful England team and in gaining a 12 point maximum, created another individual record for, added to his maximum in Poland in '74 and the one at Wembley the previous year, meant that he had been unbeaten in all three consecutive English victories — the only rider to have done so. A magnificent achievement.

It was only during the previous evening however, that Peter was riding in Belle Vue's vital League match against Sheffield. He top-scored jointly with Chris Morton and the Aces won the match by 24 points. Then he immediately flew out in a seven-seater executive jet plane from Manchester Airport to compete in that memorable Team Cup Final in Germany.

The conscientious Peter Collins would not miss that particular League encounter. And conscientiousness in speedway racing today ... plays a great part in a Champion's make-up.

Another stirring performance by Peter Collins who leads Soren Sjosten at Belle Vue in 1974

IVAN MAUGER

Ivan Mauger is not only a true professional but also a true perfectionist and he looks after his machines with meticulous attention. Surprisingly, speedway racing is the only real job he's ever had! Holding a New Zealand licence, at the age of 15, he rode on his local Aranui track in Christchurch on an old JAP.

Arriving in this country in April, 1957 at the age of 17, with his pretty young wife and a well-painted but elderly bike, his search for fame on the English raceways began. He joined Wimbledon as a raw novice and worked with the ground staff.

A perky, confident teenager, with only three months of New Zealand speedway racing behind him, it wasn't surprising that he didn't exactly set the world on fire. His Eastbourne Training School sessions proved quite tedious, and doubtless, he had the rough edges knocked off his impetuosity!

Gaining a few second-half rides at the Plough Lane circuit, he later secured the occasional reserve berth in the Dons team.

"A promising junior." That's how he was described. But he had little success and was evidently struggling hard, very hard. A little enviously, and perhaps with a certain amount of jealousy, he watched his compatriots, Ronnie Moore and Barry Briggs hitting the big time. As the season ended he returned home ... disillusioned, but still determined.

However determination and courage won in the end and by '62 the assiduous Kiwi was good enough to win the Australian Victorian Championship at Melbourne from the notable Jack Young. And, during his three years in Australia, Ivan won the Long Track Championship as well as the Victoria and Queensland State Titles.

In '63 he returned to England and linked up with Newcastle, eventually to become the team's skipper. That season he gained the Provincial League Riders' Championship, a feat he repeated the following year.

Ivan Mauger displays his expertise in an England versus New Zealand match at Belle Vue in 1973

A 1973 picture of Ivan Mauger with his grand collection of trophies, plus his "gold plated" speedway Jawa (nearly of equal fame!)

The ambitious New Zealander spent five years with Newcastle and his association culminated in a separation; he was making a clean sweep of major classics in '68 and then went on to win his first World Championship at Gothenburg. But even before his convincing victory, his brilliant gating technique had gained him countless of British League maximums, open meeting successes and Test Match appearances.

His professionalism had now reached a very high degree. For him, speedway racing was a job of work and he planned his organisation to a very fine pitch.

Relaxation is, of course, one of Ivan's secrets of success. Take for example that '69 World Final at Wembley when he arrived at the Empire Stadium with sufficient time to enjoy an afternoon's sleep! Later in the evening he gained the World Crown, once again from Barry Briggs, who was runner-up.

Then again, Ivan made speedway history in '70 when at Wroclaw, in Poland, he achieved the unique distinction of winning the World Championship for the third consecutive time, an amazing three in a row record that has never been beaten or even equalled. And the 31 year old Belle Vue teamster had won all his five heats to score a 15 point maximum, watched by a 50,000 crowd.

Winning the World 1,000 metre sand track title on two occasions was a remarkable success. Ivan's other World Final achievements were; the Title for the fourth time in '72 and second place in '73 and '74. He was British Champion four times.

Ivan left the Belle Vue team after winning three League Championships and joined Exeter in a three year contract, expiring at the end of the '75 season, for which it was reputed he was paid a fantastic five-figure amount and for good measure a car and a 'plane were thrown in!

Ivan Mauger is an honest and certainly a forthright fellow. He makes no bones about openly admitting that he races purely for the money, just to provide security for his wife and family. He still hasn't forgotten his hard times when he first came to England and found speedway in a very bad way.

Apart from his massive array of Trophies, impressive as they always are, the pride of the Mauger homestead is his gold-plated Jawa, valued at £8,000. This was the machine that won Ivan the Triple Crown at Wroclaw. Then it was gold-plated by two Americans, Ray Bokelman and George Wenn, which took eight months.

After nearly 20 years in the saddle, it could be that the illustrious Ivan Mauger has thoughts of retiring from the racing game with all the various hazards that it inevitably imposes. But, ability will be the guide-line. Whatever the future holds, the brilliant New Zealander, undoubtedly one of the world's most famous of riders, will I'm sure, almost certainly to be an integral part ... somewhere in the speedway racing scene.

MARTIN ASHBY

In all branches of life there are men who contribute in quite a big way to the success of a venture, without achieving fame, fortune, or glamour. They provide notable service, but remain comparatively obscure.

One such a man is Martin Ashby from Marlborough in Wiltshire. He's been speedway's unsung hero for many years and his notable services to the sport seemed to have been overlooked. At least they had been, until the '75 season was in its closing stages when, after being a World Finalist, and having led the English Touring Team, as captain, to superb victories in four Test Matches against Sweden, (topping the total scores) he was chosen with Malcolm Simmons, Peter Collins, John Louis and Dave Jessup to represent this country in the World Team Cup Final at Norden in West Germany. It was, perhaps, a belated acknowledgement that Martin is one of England's greatest stars. This magnificent side, on the 400 metre Halbemond track, gave a shock to the cheering British fans in the 25,000 crowd and won the contest by a big margin, amassing 41 points against Russia's 29, Sweden's 17 and Poland's 9.

But it was the under-rated quiet man of the team, Swindon skipper Martin Ashby who, thriving on International responsibility, set the seal on complete victory in heat 14 when he sped home to his third race win, which gave England a 10 point lead. It was a tremendous boost too for the new British Weslake engine, performing so brilliantly in its first-ever season, with Simmons the only English rider not riding a Weslake-engined machine.

Martin Ashby, the Swindon captain, in the British World Championship Final at Coventry in 1975

Martin's speedway career began in 1960 when, as a youngster of 15, he raced at the Aldershot circuit. Then in '61 he secured the odd second-half ride at Bristol, on one particular occasion ploughing through the safety fence, happily without injury.

Starting seriously at Blunsdon in '61, and sometimes as reserve, Martin was learning the hard way, but winning the Cornish Championship at St. Austell made life a little rosier. Luck was not always to be on his side however, for later on, a nasty crash at Norwich necessitated his neck being encased in plaster and he was in hospital for a week.

Riding as a team man in the Swindon side in '62 made Martin's full season of National League racing. Often a race-winner at Blunsdon, he missed just one single match, but nevertheless scored nearly a century of points. Then he gained his first-ever maximum at Wimbledon.

Martin's father, a former grass tracker in Wessex events, had initially built his son a miniature bike when he was only seven, but tragically that Wimbledon meeting (Swindon's last match of the season) was to be the last time he was to see his son in racing leathers. He died, all too young, on the following Boxing Day. Earlier on there had been another tragedy in the Ashby family, with the sad loss of his mother, and any less courageous fellow would have given up racing immediately. But not so with brave young Martin, still only 18. He gallantly plodded on ... with a heavy heart. With remarkable fortitude that was to be highly admired, he fought off dire distresses, just as determinedly as he had fought off his other set-backs and although a little inconsistent, he clocked up some stirring performances.

Leaving the Swindon side when the team won the British League in '67, he spent three seasons with Exeter and became a great favourite with the Devon devotees. Then it was back to Swindon, where eventually Martin took over number one spot from Barry Briggs.

Hero of many a battle, and avoiding the more serious of speedway's mishaps, he rode in every Swindon League match in '73, finishing ninth in the National averages, with 402 points. Gaining the Golden Helmet from Chris Pusey he held it for a short while until Barry Thomas took it from him at Hackney.

In retrospect, one of his personal triumphs was his second place to Ole Olsen in the prestigious British League Riders' Championship of '72. In the same event in '75 he gained a third place, after winning a run-off with John Louis, and ended a wonderful season of racing with the Golden Helmet Title.

The 32 year old star is a married man with a 2 year old son and is modest in the extreme. Now he is acknowledged as one of England's greatest shale-shifters.

And I'll always remember Martin Ashby, the introvert, as ... the King of the Quiet Men of speedway.

*Martin Ashby ends a highly
successful season in 1975 as
winner of the Golden Helmet*

CHRIS PUSEY

For sheer spectacle there has never been a rider quite like Chris Pusey, who was Britain's biggest grass track crowd-puller. That was in 1970 when he was virtually invincible. But he is a rare sight on the grass these days, owing to his heavy speedway commitments.

On leaving school, Chris's mind was made up to be a motorcycle racer. In the short time of three years, his customary blue polka-dotted helmet with resplendent technicolour leathers were known to practically every supporter on all the major grass track circuits in England. And so was his terrific riding style.

After winning the North Western Centre's 500 grass track Championship at the age of 17, he was invited by the late Dent Oliver to have a trial at Belle Vue and was subsequently given a contract. This was towards the end of the '67 season. In '68 he qualified for the semi-finals of the National Grass Track Championships but was injured at Halifax the evening before and was unable to contest the event.

Delighted with his good fortune in winning the 350cc National Title in '69, Chris said that he had achieved one ambition but that he would love to win all three class Titles. And he nearly did too, for the following year he gained the 350 and 500 Championships. He was now number two rider for Belle Vue, one of our greatest long-standing teams.

Chris Pusey of the Belle Vue Aces demonstrates his winning ways once again in the World Championship qualifying round at Sheffield in 1974

Tremendously exciting to watch, whether it be speedway or grass, Chris enjoys every minute of racing. His initial interest was such that he relinquished his first employment as a photographer to devote more time to the sport.

Sponsored by Frodsham (Cheshire) garage owner, Jim Rowlinson, young Chris in his own inimitable style, became one of the true professionals and spectacle was his speciality. Like all the rest he wasn't immune from speedway's inevitable spills. A hard and determined character, he reached the British Championship at West Ham in '70 after a frightening crash in one of the qualifying rounds. On this particular occasion his throttle had stuck open and he careered straight through the Hackney safety fence! On another occasion, at Belle Vue, he completed several somersaults, shooting twelve feet into the air and landing back on his feet!

Three time British grass Champion and the Pinhard Prize winner, a most magnificent and massive Trophy awarded annually to the rider under 21 who has made the most outstanding achievement in the field of motorcycle sport, he was selected for the young British Lions touring team for the 1970-71 Australian season. But it was in New Zealand, at Templeton speedway, in the final round of a three-match Test series, that Chris unfortunately received his most serious injuries. A fearful crash left him with a broken right thigh and a badly crushed ankle.

Flying home at the end of March he arrived just in time for his 21st birthday. Making a miraculous recovery, he was racing again at the end of July. Soon he was right back on top form and as Ivan Mauger left the Manchester side in '72, then Chris took the top slot in the Aces team, and stayed there for two seasons.

In '75, the lion-hearted fellow from Maghull, near Liverpool, and one that had taken some of speedway's hardest knocks, joined Halifax, and is still continuing his illustrious career on the shale ... at the Shay Grounds.

1975. World Championship Final at Wembley. Ole Olsen the winner with Anders Michanek (left) *runner-up and John Louis third place man*

OLE OLSEN

In the mid-1930s speedway's "Great Dane" was Morian Hansen, but today it is Ole Olsen, the 1975 World Champion. It was his second victory, for in '71 the Dane ended Ivan Mauger's unique string of World Titles and defeated the current European Champion by three points. "Ove Fundin's advice helped me to win" he remarked.

Twenty four year old Ole was the man that Ivan introduced, nursed, and coached into British League speedway. Now he was one of his greatest rivals. Just five years previous, Ole stood on the terracing at Ullevi Stadium as a very raw speedway novice, to watch his first-ever World Final. He won his first motorcycling award in '63 in a competitive event near his home town of Haderslev, when he was riding a little 175cc trials machine. Now he had proved himself in no uncertain manner to be Denmark's greatest post-war rider.

Besides winning the World Title in '71, it was a great season in other respects particularly in big individual events for the Dane was then riding in his second year for Wolverhampton after being with Newcastle since '67. His impressive achievement list included Coventry's Brandonapolis, Wimbledon's Laurels, Belle Vue's Peter Craven Memorial Trophy event, the Midland Riders' Championship, Pride of the Midland and the Olympique events (both at Wolverhampton) and the Dews Trophy event at Halifax.

For the first half of the season he held the Golden Helmet and then lost it by default to Ken McKinlay. In winning such a galaxy of top events, Ole had beaten such stars as Bengt Jansson, Barry Briggs, Ivan Mauger, Terry Betts, Bernt Persson, Eric Boocock, Ronnie Moore and Ray Wilson. But successes are often mingled with disappointments. When leading reigning Champion Ivan Mauger, an engine failure cost him the European Title at Wembley.

Scoring a one-point win over Martin Ashby, Ole won, in '72, the Division One Riders' Championship and ended the season as the Golden Helmet holder. He had successfully fought off many challengers since he initially defeated Christer Lofqvist. For the young Dane the following season was also a good one, but as far as the World Championship was concerned, he could do no better than fourth place, albeit a creditable one, riding with a damaged shoulder. Previously, he had won a host of top events, the World 1,000 metre Sand Track Final held in Norway, relegating the two West German JAP machine stars, Hans Siegl and Manfred Poschenrieder into second and third spots respectively ... the Wimbledon Laurels for the third successive time ... the Nordic Final with a stunning 15 point maximum and the Golden Sovereign event at Ipswich.

Ole was racing his first Eso machine in Denmark and as a Junior in his initial season he was practically unbeatable. 1967 saw him winning the first of four successive Danish Championships, the only rider ever to achieve this particular success.

For '71, the Danish ace was riding a brand new Eso and one that he hadn't had to buy! It was his prize for winning the Czech Golden Helmet event, a repeat performance coming four years later.

One particular afternoon of glory which Ole looks back on with immense pleasure occurred in '74 when he stormed away with the Anglo-Nordic-American Championship. This was the first major World speedway title ever staged in his Danish homeland at the Frederica circuit, with Ivan Mauger and John Louis taking second and third places.

A month later the illustrious Dane was taking part in the World Final at Ullevi. But it was not Ole's evening. Gaining two points in his first ride, he crashed heavily into the fence during a dice with Mauger in his second outing and received a bad leg injury. He was out of the Championship and out of racing for a considerable period afterwards, during which time he underwent a foot and shoulder operation.

But the superstar's determination soon brought him through and he then raced in New Zealand. Back in England in '75, 28 year old Ole continued his winning ways once again, which ended with his magnificent second World Championship success on a far from perfect track.

Ole Olsen has a great future, for age is still on his side. Married, with one young son Jakob, Ole and his very attractive wife, live in England at Holmes Chapel, in picturesque Derbyshire. Purchasing the house in '71 he commented ... "so that I can have a real go at British speedway racing this year and all the years after."

And he certainly has!

PHIL CRUMP

Phil Crump is young, very young. And, let's face it, speedway is a young man's game. At 19, this Australian journeyed to England for his initial racing season in 1971 and, linking up with Crewe, finished with a high points average. Topping Division Two averages in the ensuing year, he also won the Second Division British League Riders' Championship at Wimbledon. Unfortunately, he missed practically the entire '73 season through injury.

Joining Newport in '74 for his initial season of senior racing, Phil became a real sensation and was duly acknowledged as one of the five top riders in the country. Among his many successes, including a fantastic run of maximums, was the winning of the ornate Yorkshire TV Trophy from Ole Olsen and Peter Collins at Hull and by mid-season the Newport star had cracked four track records. Ending the season as the Golden Helmet holder, the fiery Australian returned to his home country to win the Australian Championship at the Sydney Showground circuit. He was unbeaten in his five rides, scoring a 15 point maximum. The young Victorian was using an untested engine, a new four-valve Jawa conversion with an overhead camshaft, the brain child of his fellow countryman and father-in-law, 44 year old Neil Street, the Newport skipper. It had been developed from a rough design on a piece of paper, at Christmas!

A thrilling study of Phil Crump in a terrific tussle with Bernt Persson (almost hidden) and Gordeev

Phil's tremendous racing ability, his more mature riding, plus his new motor, took him to a host of honours. He cracked three track records which included the coveted Mildura Park speedway record, previously held by Ivan Mauger.

His amazing form in Australia provided the backbone of his successful team's contests in the Test Matches against the British Lions and he was top scorer. He then proceeded to win his country's new National Long Track Championship with a devastating performance at Tailem in South Australia. And Phil and Neil had the two fastest Jawas in the country.

Returning to England in '75 with their new-engined models, the two amazed everyone by consistently reeling off maximum after maximum points. Then Phil won the £500 Spring Classic at Wimbledon in superb style when, at this particular meeting, to be ahead at the first bend was essential on the rain-sodden track. With a session of meteoric starts, Phil made the gate four times out of five, leaving his other 15 rivals, all top riders, completely smothered in slimy shale! It was no less than a magnificent performance. This was the Australian Champion's initial major success in England.

Later, in the World Championship Final at Wembley, on a very poor track, the dynamic Australian gained a creditable joint fifth place with Peter Collins and Malcolm Simmons. Later still, he added a second place in the British League Riders' Championship.

As I have said, Phil Crump is a young man. His terrier-like track ferocity inevitably makes him tremendously popular wherever he rides. If Lady Luck stays on his side, he will have many, many more years in the sport. But should he make an early retirement, he will have already earned a niche in the Hall of speedway racing fame.

The magnificent England Team which won the World Team Cup Final at Norden. From left to right; top row, *Jack Fearnley, Dave Jessup, Malcolm Simmons* and *Len Silver.* Bottom row, *Peter Collins, Martin Ashby* and *John Louis*

Here's tremendous action! At Norden's 1975 World Team Cup Final (West Germany), from left to right, *Valeri Gordeev (USSR), Bernt Persson (Sweden), Marek Cieslak (Poland)* and *Malcolm Simmons (England)*

DAVE JESSUP

Dave Jessup, a young superstar, jumped from a novice to Champion in just two seasons! His amazingly fast ride to the top started in '69, when he was making a big name for himself as the youngest rider in speedway. This was at Eastbourne's Second Division circuit, where racing had been re-established after a long lapse. The 16 year old dark-haired lad made many meritorious performances, but previously he had begun his competitive motorcycling career with a junior grass track club in Kent.

In 1970, still with Eastbourne, his further rise was such that Dave was making an increasing number of appearances with First Division Wembley. With great delight he went on to a worthy win in the Division Two Riders' Championship and he also appeared in the Young England Test team.

Joining the Leicester team at the start of the '73 season, and riding as number one for the Lions, he immediately became a big favourite at the Blackbird Road circuit. But, unhappily, he was soon to be side-lined after injuring his left knee in a spill on his home track.

By virtue of his third place in the '74 British speedway Final, Dave now competed in his first World Championship Final at Ullevi, but could only muster a disappointing five points. Nothing seemed to go right for him that evening and he disliked the deep, rough track. Nevertheless, at 21, he had reached a World Final, which, owing to its very nature was certainly a feat in itself — something that hundreds of riders have never accomplished. That was of some consolation.

Mastering the abominal track condition in beautiful style, the Leicester star crowned an immensely successful season with a superb performance at Wimbledon, to win the famous Laurels meeting.

Then in July, '75, Dave won the London Riders' Championship, after which he had a crack at the Golden Helmet competition, with Ole Olsen as his rival. An intriguing tussle potentially, but it turned out otherwise. Riding brilliantly and still maintaining his fine form, the Leicester international surprisingly won the match at Wolverhampton 2-0, but the return at Leicester ended in a fiasco. Dave won the first race and then Ole was excluded in race two for exceeding the two minute rule and the former was acclaimed the winner. But Dave was not happy. "That was not the way I wanted to win the Golden Helmet" he remarked.

Like Malcolm Simmons, Dave Jessup loves a spot of trials riding in the winter and oddly enough, they ride similar machines, a 250cc Ossa. "Trials riding allows one to let off steam, in fact it's great fun and not so much of a rat race" says the very likeable David Jessup ... just 23 years old.

Exhibiting all his customary flair, Dave Jessup speeds on to yet another victory. He was transferred to Reading in early 1976 for a record transfer-fee of £4,500

JOHN LOUIS

They call him "Tiger." That's the ever-smiling John Louis, who piloted his new all-British Weslake-engined machine triumphantly into third spot after a run-off with Ivan Mauger in the 1975 World Championship Final. It was staged, surprisingly, on a poorly-prepared circuit which certainly failed to live up to the Wembley tradition.

John's notable third placing made him the highest-placed Englishman in the 13 previous Finals, ever since the late Peter Craven won the crown in 1962, and he was highly delighted to stand on the winners' rostrum alongside the victor Ole Olsen and second-man Anders Michanek. But it wasn't his first World Championship Final. He had come fourth in both '72 and '74.

At Brandon, John, with five unbeaten rides, became the British Champion for the first time and needless to say, he was very jubilant over this particular success. It was also a Weslake supershow with Weslakes taking, first, second, fourth and fifth places. It should be remembered that only a few months previous, John was thrashing the new four-valver prototype in an exhausting but successful shale debut around the Hackney track, touching 8,000 peak revs., on the straights and thus displaying the prodigious power of the new motor. Apart from the JAP, no engine had ever been so successful in open competition so quickly after its initiation.

One can hardly realise that John did not enter into speedway until the middle of the 1969 season, and therefore he is, comparatively, a newcomer to the game. But in the 6½ years he has been racing, every one has been packed with action.

Initially, John began his motorcycling competition career by riding in scrambles on a 250cc Dot. Then came a 250cc Greeves and he gained the 1969 Eastern Centre Scrambles Championship (250cc class). He had already struck up a friendship with Dave Bickers, a European Motocross Champion and the local motorcycle agent at Ipswich, who sponsored him on CZ machines. Dave was his employer for some four years.

The World Champion, Anders Michanek wins the Daily Express Trophy in 1974 with Terry Betts (right) *runner up and Bengt Jansson who was third*

Speedwaywise, John had seen the racing at Ipswich in '68 as a 23 year old interested spectator. Later he had a trial spin around the Foxall Heath circuit. Then came some second-half rides and his appetite, once whetted, craved for more. He attended Olle Nygren's training school and, with his natural aptitude it wasn't long before John became the top rider in Ipswich's Second Division team. After winning the Division Two British Riders' Championship in '71, he found himself, still with Ipswich, in senior racing the following season and from then on there was no stopping "Tiger" John. He became captain of his side.

As the years went by the superstar's successes came thick and fast ... and track records too, for in '75 he held the records at Hackney, Leicester, Wimbledon, Coventry, Bradford, Ipswich and Rye House! His World Team Cup performances have been very impressive, but these apart, he has enjoyed his Golden Helmet tussles, especially in '74, when he successfully fought off challenges by Ray Wilson, Peter Collins, Malcolm Simmons, Dag Lovas and Ole Olsen, only to relinquish the title to Newport's Phil Crump.

It is not surprising that John Louis, with his immense likeability, is such a popular fellow. Patriotism plays a substantial part in his make-up and, riding with British Weslake engines that enable him to create such amazing performances, pleases him greatly.

1975. Third in the World Championship. That was a superb and heroic piece of work but his best is probably yet to come.

John Louis, pioneer user of the Weslake speedway engine, leads Peter Collins and Alan Wilkinson in an exciting Belle Vue versus Ipswich match

ANDERS MICHANEK

The 1975 Swedish Champion, that dark, good-looking Swede from Stockholm, originally came to England to link up with the Long Eaton team in 1967. He had, of course, been racing in his home country for two seasons with the Gararna Second Division side, but here he was relatively unknown.

For several seasons quiet man Anders struggled to reach the top. At times he doubted his own ability to such an extent that he was once on the point of giving up the game. But he courageously battled on. As the seasons went by he gradually improved; it was a methodical ascent.

Then came '73. Even at the beginning of the season it became evident that Anders meant business, real business. Winning the Spring Classic Trophy at Wimbledon was followed by a scintillating display at Hackney to annex a star-studded Superama and then he took the runner-up spot in Wimbledon's Internationale. He then added the Nordic/British Title to his ever-growing list of successes whilst at the same time he was leading his team (Reading) to an eventual victory in the British League Championship. Anders had certainly struck his greatest form, and after taking the European Title at Abensberg (West Germany) he was, not surprisingly, the favourite for the World Championship.

The Swedish ace went on to win the Blue Riband Title at Poole, the Golden Gauntlets event at Leicester despite a severe attack of influenza, the Peter Arnold Memorial Trophy, the Battle of Britain Trophy and the Manpower Championship, all at Reading.

After all these monumental efforts it was now the Mighty Michanek, or Michanek the Magnificent. These big speedway occasions emphasised the man's unflappable temperament. Now came the World Final at Chorzow in Poland. Excluded once for tape-breaking, Anders could only clock up tenth position. Disappointed to a degree, the likeable Swede was, nevertheless, enjoying a remarkable season, his best-ever in fact. Which was, perhaps, some consolation for his low World Final score of only six points. Even so, there was always another year.

Married in '73 to a very attractive girl, Margarita, Anders — a keep-fit addict — commented: "In every way it has been my most wonderful year."

Banned, like his compatriots too, by the BSPA from British League racing in '74, "Mich" was able to take a comparatively easier life, but the superstar's devastating form remained. With Soren Sjosten as partner, they won the World Pairs Championship for Sweden at Belle Vue. Then in September came the World Championship Final at Gothenburg. It would be Anders seventh attempt. Cool, calm and confident and exhibiting all his customary flair he gave a truly magnificent display of classic riding that gave Sweden its first World Champion for seven years. Watched by a record 40,000 crowd, the Swede rode inexorably to victory in five immaculate rides and broke the track record three times! He was the supreme and complete master of the Ullevi circuit and his performance made the Swedish crowd rock with wild delight.

I have always admired the very modest Anders Michanek. But after the new World Champion told a captive audience of Press men as congratulations were showered upon him: "There's more in life than money and Speedway," I admired him even more.

They live in memory

Joe Abbott: Cyril Anderson: Charlie Appleby: Jack Biggs: Charlie Blacklock: Con Cantwell: Norman Clay: Clem Cort: Geoff Curtis: Reg Craven: Peter Craven: Fritz Dirtl: Eric Dunn: Ray Duggan: Jack Eaves: Roy Eather: Harry Eyre: Malcolm Flood: Tom Farndon: Norman Gillespie: "Buzz" Hibberd: Bob Hibbert: Gerald Hussey: Stan Hart: Alan Hunt: Jack Ladd: Ken Le Breton: Lionel Levy; Max Pearce: Gary Petersen: Ernie Roccio: Mike Rogers: Ernie Rawlins: Ted Stevens: "Aussie" Rosenfeld: Jock Shead: Jack Sharp: Ray Sharp: Johnny Thompson: Tadeusz Teodorowicz: Jack Unstead: Reg Vigor: Dave Wills: Bill Wilson: "Broncho" Wilson: Noel Watson ... and the others.

SPEEDWAY RACING CAN BE TERRIBLY CRUEL AT TIMES. These brave riders gave their lives to the sport they loved so well.

TO REMIND YOU OF THE RISK THE RIDERS RUN ...

Here is a superb action picture of the 'Wizard of Balance', PETER CRAVEN, — twice World Champion — who lost his life at Edinburgh Speedway in 1963.

Left, *Con Cantwell (an Australian killed in Belgium in the thirties)*
Right, *Tom Farndon (British Individual Speedway Champion died from injuries at New Cross in 1935)*
Centre, *Buzz Hibberd (an Australian killed at Sydney in the thirties)*

Right, *Reg Vigor (22-years-old died from injuries received at Wimbledon in 1937)*
Left, *Ken Le Breton (died after a crash at Sydney in 1951)*

Joe Abbot (died from injuries received at Odsal in 1950, then the oldest speedway rider)

Gery Peterson (the Wolverhampton teamster)

Postscript

Neil Cameron's bike takes the upper hand as he climbs all over King's Lynn's Barry Crowson at Wimbledon in 1974

The dynamic Polish rider, Zenon Plech comes a cropper in front of the Australian John Titman. A 1974 picture

Tom Owen (no 1) crashes into the fence with Steve Wilcocks in a Bradford versus Newcastle match